DEONTIC LOGIC:

A Comprehensive Appraisal and
a New Proposal

Azizah al-Hibri

Copyright © 1978 by

University Press of America, Inc.™

4710 Auth Place, S.E., Washington, D.C. 20023

All rights reserved

Printed in the United States of America

ISBN: 0-8191-0303-9

Library of Congress Catalog Card Number: 78-66422

DEDICATION

To my grandfather
M. Toufic El-Hibri
The first teacher of philosophy I ever had.

PREFACE

The present work is a modification of my dissertation, written under the supervision of the Philosophy Department at The University of Pennsylvania. During that time I received helpful suggestions and criticisms from Brian Chellas, Zolton Domotor and James Garson. I appreciate their assistance, especially as it has enabled me to provide a more comprehensive version of the leading themes. Any errors of omission, of course, are mine alone.

One theme not discussed is a critique of time-bound views of deontic logic. I am preparing such a critique for publication at a future time.

Azizah Cox

TABLE OF CONTENTS

CHAPTER	PAGE

I. INTRODUCTION 1

    1. A Brief History of Deontic Logic 1
    2. Some Comments on the Paradoxes of Deontic Logic 2
    3. The Scope and Method of the Study 3
    4. A Brief Preview of the Contributions of the Author 5
    Footnotes 7

II. THE BASIC PRINCIPLES AND PARADOXES OF VON WRIGHT'S OLD SYSTEM OF DEONTIC LOGIC 9

    1. von Wright's Old System of Deontic Logic 9

        a. Introductory Remarks 9
        b. The Axioms and Rules of the Old System 10
        c. The Rule (R3) 11
        d. Some Results of the Modified System 12

    2. Some Arguments for Rejecting (A3) 14
    3. Some Arguments in Favor of the Basic Principles of SDL⁻ 16

        a. The Principle that Consequences of what Ought to be the Case Ought to be the Case 16
        b. The Principle that Ought-Statements do not Conflict 18
        c. The Principle that "Ought" Implies "Can" 18

    4. An Explication of the Notion of "Paradox" as Used in Deontic Logic 20
    5. The Paradoxes of Deontic Logic 22

        a. Ross' Paradox 22
        b. Åqvist's Paradox 23
        c. The Good Samaritan Paradox 23
        d. The Robber's Paradox 24
        e. The Victim's Paradox 24
        f. Plato's Paradox 24
        g. Sartre's Paradox 25

   h. The Paradox of the Contrary-to-Duty
     Imperative 26
   i. The Epistemic Obligation Paradox 28

  6. Sorting the Paradoxes of Deontic Logic into
    Three Main Groups 29
  7. The General Lines for Resolving the
    Paradoxes 31
 Footnotes 32

III. RESOLUTIONS OF THE FIRST TWO GROUPS OF DEONTIC
   PARADOXES 37

 A. A Resolution of the First Group of
   Paradoxes in Deontic Logic 37

  1. On the Relation between (DR1) and
    Ross' Paradox 37
  2. Beatty's Argument against One Version
    of (DR1) 38
  3. Response to Beatty 39
  4. Solution to Ross' Paradox 40
  5. The Various Proposed Solutions to the
    Good Samaritan Paradox 41
  6. Solution to the Good Samaritan
    Paradox 42

 B. A Resolution of the Second Group of
   Paradoxes in Deontic Logic 45

  1. A Proposed Resolution of Plato's
    Paradox 45
  2. The Notions of "Actual" and "*Prima
    Facie*" Obligations and their Role
    in Plato's Paradox 46
  3. An Examination of Some Arguments
    against the Principle that "Ought"
    Implies "Can" 50

   a. Lemmon's Arguments 50
   b. Hare's Arguments 52

  4. An Exploration of Castañeda's Method
    for Solving Plato's Paradox 54
  5. Criticism of Castañeda's Method 56
  6. The Special Significance of Sartre's
    Paradox 59

7. Some General Observations Concerning *Prima Facie* and Actual Ought-Statements ... 61

    a. The Moral Weight of an Ought-Statement ... 61
    b. The Role of Circumstances in Determining Obligations ... 62

8. The Complexity of Determining an Actual Ought-Statement on the Basis of *Prima Facie* Ones ... 64

    a. Considerations of the Situation as a Whole May Rebut all the *Prima Facie* Ought-Statements Related to that Situation ... 65
    b. Considerations of the Situation as a Whole May Lead to a Moral Agent to Change the Situation ... 67

9. Solution to the Second Group of Paradoxes ... 68

    a. Plato's Paradox ... 69
    b. Sartre's Paradox ... 69

10. Other Proposed Solutions for the Second Group of Paradoxes ... 72

    a. van Fraassen's Solution ... 72
    b. Hintikka's Solution ... 76
    c. von Wright's Solution ... 78
    d. Segerberg's Solution ... 81

11. Some Concluding Remarks about *Prima Facie* and Actual Obligations ... 82

Footnotes ... 84

IV. A RESOLUTION OF THE LAST GROUP OF PARADOXES ... 89

1. A Study of the Contrary-to-Duty Imperative Paradox ... 89
2. Proposed Solutions to this Paradox ... 90

    a. Hintikka's Solution ... 90
    b. Åqvist's Solution ... 91
    c. von Wright's Solution ... 94
    d. Mott's Solution ... 95

3. Solution to the Paradox 97
Footnotes 98

V. THE LOGICAL SYSTEM S 101

1. The Foundation of S 101
2. The Syntax of S 102
3. Axiom Schemas and Rules of Inference for S 102
4. Some Serived Rules and a Theorem for S 105
5. Semantics for S 107

a. A Model for S 107
b. Restrictions on R 108
c. Some Definitions 109
d. The Notion of Truth at α in m 110
e. Some Additional Definitions 111

6. The Soundness of S 111

a. A2 iv Valid 111
b. A3 is Valid 112
c. A4 is Valid 112
d. R1 Preserves Validity 113
e. R2 Preserves Validity 114
f. The Soundness of S has been Established 115

7. The Completeness of S 115

a. A Sketch of the Completeness Proof for S 115
b. The Canonical Model m 116
c. R in the Canonical Model Satisfies the Restrictions Specified in Section 5.b of this Chapter 117
d. A Theorem about m 119
e. The Completeness Theorem for S 119

8. Formulas and Rules not Derivable in S 123

a. Formulas and Rules that are Independent of S 123
b. Formulas that are Inconsistent with S 125

Footnotes 126

VI. SYSTEMS S_1, S_2, AND ALTERNATIVE SEMANTICS FOR S   129

    A. Systems S_1 and S_2 129
        1. Some Additional Axioms   129
        2. Additional Restrictions on R   130
        3. S_1 and S_2 are Sound   131
    B. Alternative Semantics for S   134
        1. O(~A/A)   134

            a. Two Different Points of View   135
            b. Hansson's Argument against
                O(~A/A)   135

                (1) The First Reading and
                    Hansson's Notion of
                    "Undoing"   136
                (2) The Second Reading and the
                    Extra Meaning in O(~A/A)   136
                (3) Some Comments on the Second
                    Reading and our Notion of
                    "Undoing"   137
                (4) The Third Reading and Temporal
                    Specifications   138
                (5) A Criticism of the Third
                    Reading   139
                (6) Hansson's Argument has other
                    Consequences   140

        2. Lewis' Semantics   141
        3. van Fraassen's Semantics for LC   144
        4. Other Approaches   146

            a. The Imperatival Approach   146
            b. The Åqvist-type Approach   147
    Footnotes   148

VII. CONCLUSION   151

    1. A Brief Evaluation of the Various Deontic
        Logics   151

        a. von Wright's Systems   151
        b. Hintikka's System   152
        c. Åqvist's System   154
        d. Hansson's Systems   155

	e. Segerberg's System	155
	f. Lewis' System	156
	g. van Fraassen's Systems	156
	h. Mott's System	158
2.	A Brief Evaluation of S	158
3.	A Summary Statement on the Value of this Work	160
4.	Suggestions for Further Research	161
Footnotes		162

APPENDICES

1	165
2	167
3	169

CHAPTER I

INTRODUCTION

1. A Brief History of Deontic Logic

Deontic logic, also referred to as the logic of obligation, is a relatively new branch of logic.[1] The first attempt at constructing a formal system of deontic logic was made by Ernst Mally in 1926.[2] Since then, several attempts followed, of which the most notable is that of G. H. von Wright in his classic paper "Deontic Logic", published in 1951.[3] Von Wright's paper prompted a lot of reaction in the field and has influenced work in deontic logic ever since.[4]

The axioms suggested by von Wright in his paper, together with one additional axiom introduced by other logicians later on, constitute what is generally referred to as standard deontic logic.[5] In recent years standard deontic logic has been questioned by many philosophers, including von Wright himself in his paper, "A Correction to a New System of Deontic Logic."[6] Consequently, several of von Wright's original axioms were rejected and new ones were proposed.[7] One reason for this recent trend is the philosopher's mounting concern about a set of paradoxes that appeared in deontic logic as early as 1941 and culminated in Chisholm's paper, "Contrary-to-Duty Imperatives and Deontic Logic", published in 1963.[8] These paradoxes are discussed at length in Chapters II, III and IV of this work. More recently a new trend in deontic logic has come to the surface.[9] It was prompted by the development of conditional logic, as well as by von Wright's paper, "A New System of Deontic Logic".[10] The new trend pronounced as sound most of the principles on which the axioms of standard deontic logic rest. But it acknowledged that the axioms as formulated originally by von Wright led to paradoxes. It is maintained within this trend that a new notion must be introduced in order to handle a major paradox of deontic logic, the paradox of the Contrary-to-Duty Imperative, which we discuss in Chapters II and IV.[11] The new notion is that of

1

conditional obligation. It is regarded by some as a complex notion based on two different logics: conditional logic and deontic logic.[12] Others have regarded it as a simple notion requiring the introduction of a dyadic deontic operator.[13] It is worth noting here that several attempts at utilizing the notion of conditional obligation appeared also within the earlier trend. The notion in this case was put in the service of arguments attacking standard deontic logic and supplying a different solution to the above-mentioned paradoxes.[14] Today the issues surrounding von Wright's standard deontic logic are still highly controversial. The new round of debate concerning the fundamental axioms of deontic logic has become more sophisticated, but it is still far from having settled the old issues that were raised by von Wright.

2. Some Comments on the Paradoxes of Deontic Logic

The paradoxes of deontic logic are not paradoxes in the strict sense. In Chapter II, we explicate precisely what is meant by a paradox in deontic logic. We also exhibit these paradoxes and the principles on which they are based. Basically, there are four hosts of paradoxes in deontic logic. They are represented by what is generally known as (1) Ross' paradox, (2) the Good Samaritan paradox, (3) the Conflict-of-Duty paradox, and (4) the paradox of the Contrary-to-Duty Imperative.

The corresponding principles involved are (1) the principle of disjunctive obligation, (2) the principle that the consequence of what is obligatory is also obligatory, (3) the principle that obligations do not conflict and (4) the principle that no one is obligated to do the impossible, i.e., "ought" implies "can". As we shall see in Chapters II and III, the first two principles are closely related and are both involved in the first two paradoxes listed above. Similarly, we shall see in Chapters II, III and IV that the last two principles are also closely related and are both involved in the last two paradoxes.

A preliminary discussion establishing the

plausibility of these paradoxes is introduced in Chapter II, so that the reader may appreciate the seriousness of the problems that have worried philosophers in deontic logic. It will also become clear in the same chapter that principles (1)-(4) are expressed by those axioms of standard deontic logic that were introduced by von Wright. Hence, resolving the paradoxes which involve these principles is crucial for determining the essential features of a basic deontic logic.

3. The Scope and Method of the Study

As we mentioned in Section 2, Chapter II is concerned with presenting von Wright's original deontic system, as well as the paradoxes of deontic logic that were generated from these principles. Arguments are presented to establish the initial plausibility of both the principles and the paradoxes. In the first part of Chapter III, we discuss Ross' paradox and the Good Samaritan paradox. We also supply a historically condensed preview of the proposed solutions. Our own solutions are developed and these paradoxes are disposed of in this chapter.

Our solution to Ross' paradox rests on the observation that it can be formulated only in isolation from the totality of our deontic system. Furthermore, it is paradoxical only in light of the deontic system from which we isolated it. This observation about the interconnection between the paradox and the deontic system leads directly to the resolution of the paradox.

On the other hand, the Good Samaritan paradox is resolved by arguing that it is based on an old modal ambiguity - the ambiguity of the scope of the deontic operator O . Once that ambiguity is cleared, the paradox is resolved.

The second part of Chapter III centers on the Conflict-of-Duty paradox. This paradox is regarded by the author as the most crucial paradox in deontic logic. For this reason the paradox is developed with great care. Two notions that are crucial for an adequate solution of this paradox are introduced. The two notions are those of prima facie ought-statements and actual ought-statements. These notions were originally introduced by Sir David Ross.[15] In this work we develop the notions further and discuss the complexity of the relation of these notions to each other.

The two notions are then used to resolve the Conflict-of-Duty paradox and our solution is later compared with the solutions that have been proposed by other philosophers. Our detailed discussion of the paradox and subsequent solution will make it easier to spot the confusion on which some of the proposed solutions to this paradox are based.

In particular, we shall discuss a proposed solution to the Conflict-of-Duty paradox based on the rejection of an important deontic principle, namely, the principle of detachment. Our discussion will vindicate this important principle and show that the argument against it is based on a confusion between the notions of prima facie and actual ought-statements.

In Chapter IV, we show how our resolution of the Conflict-of-Duty paradox brings about the paradox of the Contrary-to-Duty Imperative. Again, an evaluation of the various attempts at resolving this paradox is undertaken. This paradox is also quite important since it justifies, according to our results in Chapter IV, the introduction of a dyadic deontic operator, that of conditional obligation, $O(/)$.

As we stated earlier, the appearance of paradoxes in deontic logic has led historically to the rejection of one or more principles on which that logic is based. Therefore, by examining these paradoxes and disposing of them in our work, we are eliminating a major motivation for rejecting this logic. Furthermore, the process of examining and resolving these paradoxes, reveals at the same time the intuitiveness of the principles of standard deontic logic. The confusions on which many of these criticisms are based are also revealed. Hence, the case for standard deontic logic will be made in this work through the study of these paradoxes.

In Chapters V, VI and VII, we systematize the results of the earlier chapters. A system S is introduced with the appropriate semantics and completeness proof. By then, most of the axioms of the system S will have been defended. The remaining ones are discussed and motivated. Interesting theorems are exhibited.

It must be pointed out that although the system S includes all the intuitive principles of standard deontic logic, it is not a minimal system of that logic. We have chosen to include in S what we consider to be a major deontic principle, namely the principle of detachment. This single departure from a minimal standard deontic logic is justified by the fundamental character of the principle in question. Though this principle has been regarded with suspicion by many philosophers, its intuitiveness was also stressed by others.[16] In this work, we show that the suspicions concerning this principle are unfounded. Therefore, the principle of detachment is introduced as an axiom of S.

The semantics used for S is based on the notion of a possible world. Thus, the truth of a sentence $O(A/C)$ at a possible world α will be defined in terms of a set of possible worlds where A is true, and which are related to C and to α in a certain way. Therefore, this set of worlds can be regarded as supplying a moral standard to the world α at which $O(A/C)$ is true. The intuitiveness of this semantics will be defended in this work, although other semantics, like those proposed by David Lewis and Bas van Fraassen will also be considered.[17] Furthermore, S will be compared to other deontic systems showing its advantages over them. Finally, some suggestions will be made about possible additions to and enrichments of S.

4. A Brief Preview of the Contributions of the Author

a. It is clear from the discussion in Section 3 that this study purports to resolve the major paradoxes that have appeared in deontic logic. In doing so, it shall present new arguments concerning the four principles listed in Section 2. The arguments will vindicate these principles and lend support to the view that a conditionalized deontic logic, which preserves their truth, is adequate for capturing our deontic intuitions without being open to paradoxes. The work exhibits this logic and points out in detail its important features. In the process, various well-known views are presented and criticized.

    b. The solution to the Conflict-of-Duty paradox is doubly significant. Not only does the solution vindicate principle (3), that obligations do not conflict, and consequently, the related principle (4), that "ought" implies "can", but it does something else which is of major importance to deontic logic. It provides a fresh perspective which casts the basic disagreements in deontic logic in a new light. While it was often assumed that the philosophers representing different trends in deontic logic have been proposing competing logics, our results in the second part of Chapter III will establish that these logics when properly understood do not compete. They treat basically of two different notions, one of which does not belong to the domain of deontic logic proper.

    The introduction of these two notions results also in clearing the confusion surrounding an important deontic principle, namely, the principle of detachment.

    c. Finally, this study concludes by presenting a new paradox-free conditional deontic logic S which is sound and complete. The system S is standard in the sense that it preserves all the principles that were proposed in von Wright's original system.

    It also satisfies all of the criteria developed in the body of this work for evaluating deontic logics. As we shall see in Chapter VII, not one of the well-known deontic logics satisfies all these criteria.

Footnotes

Chapter I

[1] See, for example, Hector-Neri Castañeda, "The Logic of Obligation," Philosophical Studies 10 (1950), 62-75.

[2] Ernst Mally, Grundgesetze des Sollens. Elemente der Logik des Willens, (Graz: Leuschner & Lubensky, 1926).

[3] Georg Henrik von Wright, "Deontic Logic," Mind 60 (1951), 1-15.

[4] See, for example, Bas van Fraassen, "The Logic of Conditional Obligation," Journal of Philosophical Logic 1, (1972), 417-438. Also see Bengt Hansson, "An Analysis of Some Deontic Logics," in Deontic Logic: Introductory and Systematic Readings, ed. Risto Hilpinen (New York: Humanities Press, 1971), 121-147.

[5] Dagfinn Føllesdal and Risto Hilpinen, "Deontic Logic: An Introduction," Hilpinen, 13.

[6] von Wright, "A Correction to a New System of Deontic Logic," Danish Yearbook of Philosophy 2 (1965), 103-107. Also see van Fraassen, "Values and the Heart's Command," Journal of Philosophy 70 (1973), 5.

[7] Cf. van Fraassen, "Conditional Obligation," and Hansson.

[8] See Alf Ross, "Imperatives and Logic," Theoria 7 (1941), 53-71. See also Roderick Chisholm, "Contrary-to-Duty Imperatives and Deontic Logic," Analysis 24 (1963), 33-36.

[9] See, for example, Peter L. Mott, "On Chisholm's Paradox," Journal of Philosophical Logic 2 (1973), 197-211.

[10] von Wright, "A New System of Deontic Logic," Danish Yearbook of Philosophy 1 (1964), 173-182.

[11] See, for example, Mott.

[12] See, for example, Brian F. Chellas, "Conditional

Obligation," <u>Logical Theory and Semantical Analysis:
Essays Dedicated to Stig Kanger on his Fiftieth
Birthday</u>, ed. Soren Stenlund, (Dordrecht: D. Reidel
Publishing Co., 1974), 23-33.

[13] See, for example, van Fraassen, "Conditional Obligation."

[14] See, for example, van Fraassen, "Values," 5-19. Also, see for example, Hansson.

[15] See, for example, W. David Ross, <u>Foundations of Ethics</u> (Oxford: The Clarendon Press, 1951), 84-86.

[16] See, for example, van Fraassen, "The Logic of Conditional Obligation," 422, and Jaakko Hintikka, "Some Main Problems of Deontic Logic," Hilpinen, 91.

[17] See Section IV:B:9.

CHAPTER II

THE BASIC PRINCIPLES AND PARADOXES OF VON
WRIGHT'S OLD SYSTEM OF DEONTIC LOGIC

1. von Wright's Old System of Deontic Logic[1]

   a. Introductory Remarks. In 1951, G. H. von Wright introduced the basis of what later came to be known as the standard system of deontic logic (SDL).[2] The system as introduced by von Wright was based on the notion of permission as a deontic primitive.[3] Since that date almost all deontic logicians have chosen the notion of obligation as their deontic primitive.[4] All logicians in the field, including von Wright, hold that the notions of obligation and permission are interdefinable in the following manner:[5]

(0) (a) A is obligatory if and only if it is not the case that it is permitted that not-A;

   (b) A is permitted if and only if it is not the case that it is obligatory that not-A.

thus one can easily restate von Wright's basic axioms for SDL in terms of the notion of obligation. But in order to attain some accuracy in stating these axioms we first define the system SDL. The system has unlimited supply of variables A, B, ... Those variables were defined by von Wright as "schematic descriptions of a type of proposition-like entity" which he calls "generic states of affairs." More recently, philosophers have defined these variables as ranging over sentences, propositions, or even acts.[7] In this study, the variables will be defined as ranging over sentences. This is in accordance with one of the trends already existing in the literature. It also permits us to base deontic logic on propositional logic. The truth-functional connectives are $\sim$, $\wedge$, $\vee$, $\leftarrow$, $\leftrightarrow$, for negation, conjunction, disjunction, material implication, and material equivalence. The system also has a unary logical operator O, and brackets.

We can now restate definition (b) formally. The notion of permission here is a derivative notion expressed in the system by a unary operator P defined in accordance with (O) as follows:

(b')   PA = ~ O ~ A.

    b. The Axioms and Rules of the Old System. We are now ready to introduce von Wright's system. He states that his system has the following two axioms and four rules of inference:[8]

(A1) ⊢ ~(OA∧O~A)

(A2) ⊢ O(A∧B) ↔ (OA∧OB)

The rules of inference are:

(R1) and (R2) These are the usual rules for substitution of variables and for modus ponens.

(R3) A variable or molecular compound of variables in an axiom or theorem may be replaced by a tautologically equivalent compound of variables.

(R4) The O-expression which is obtained from a tautology of propositional logic by replacing its propositional variables by O-expressions is a theorem.

    In the statement of rules above, von Wright refers to theorems. The notion of "theorem" will be defined rigorously in Section IV:6.e. We define the notion here informally as follows: A theorem A of a system K, symbolically ⊢ A , is either an axiom of K, or can be obtained from one or more axioms of K by the rules of inference of the system K.

    In the next section we shall speak of two compounds of variables as "provably equivalent." We define this notion now. Two compounds of variables are provably equivalent if and only if their biconditional is a theorem. That is, A is provably equivalent to A' if and only if ⊢ A↔A'.

Finally, in the proof of the theorem listed below and in other proofs, we justify some of our deductions by appealing to classical propositional logic. In each case, this is possible because the system within which the proof is being conducted contains classical propositional logic as a fragment. In the case of von Wright's Old System, this is guaranteed by (R1), (R2) and (R4).

c. The Rule (R3). It should be noted that (R3) permits the replacement of tautological equivalents only. Consequently, if a variable or compound of variables is not tautologically equivalent to another, but is provably equivalent to it, it may not replace it. For example, where A is atomic, OA and O∼∼A are provably equivalent by (R3), i.e., ⊢ OA↔O∼∼A. But OA and O∼∼A are not tautologically equivalent. Hence, a statement like OOA↔OO∼∼A is not provable because we may not replace OA by O∼∼A. Consequently, our logical intuitions require a less restrictive rule of replacement than (R3):

(R3') A variable or molecular compound of variables in an axiom or theorem may be replaced by a provably equivalent compound of variables.

The reader must not hasten to conclude that von Wright's system has a serious problem which is to be solved by replacing (R3) by (R3'). The criticism against (R3) carries weight in light of our move to define variables as ranging over sentences. Since the deontic operation O attaches to sentences and produces in its turn sentences, iteration of O is possible. Hence, when expressions like OOA arise we face the problem described above in the absence of a rule like (R3').

On the other hand, von Wright's variables range, as we stated earlier, over "generic states of affairs." The deontic operation O attaches to these generic states of affairs and produces propositions. Consequently, expressions like OOA are not well-formed. Also, expressions like A→OA are not well-formed either. Therefore, under these conditions (R3) is an adequate rule of the system.

Since we have chosen earlier to let our variables range over sentences, we replace (R3) by (R3'). In the following section we shall exhibit a derived rule and a theorem of the resulting system. We note that the theorem is provable in von Wright's Old System also.

    d. Some Results of the Modified System. We shall now list one derived rule and one theorem of this system.

(DR1) $\quad \dfrac{\vdash A \rightarrow B}{\vdash OA \rightarrow OB}$

We assume that $\vdash A \rightarrow B$. By propositional logic, this means that $\vdash (A \wedge B) \leftrightarrow A$. By (R3'), it follows that $\vdash O(A \wedge B) \leftrightarrow OA$. Hence, by (A2) and propositional logic, $\vdash OA \leftrightarrow (OA \wedge OB)$. Therefore, $\vdash OA \rightarrow OB$. Q.E.D.

Theorem T_0.

    Each of (1)-(10) is a theorem.

(1) $O(A \rightarrow B) \rightarrow (OA \rightarrow OB)$

(2) $(OA \vee OB) \rightarrow O(A \vee B)$

(3) $\sim O(A \wedge \sim A)$

(4) $OA \rightarrow PA$

(5) $[OA \wedge O[(A \wedge B) \rightarrow C]] \rightarrow O(B \rightarrow C)$

(6) $P(A \vee B) \leftrightarrow (PA \vee PB)$

(7) $P(A \wedge B) \rightarrow (PA \wedge PB)$

(8) $[PA \wedge O(A \rightarrow B)] \rightarrow PB$

(9) $[O(A \rightarrow (B \vee C)) \wedge \sim PB \wedge \sim PC] \rightarrow \sim PA$

(10) $\sim [O(A \vee B) \wedge \sim PA \wedge \sim PB]$

    Clauses (1)-(4) are important for later discussions in this work. Hence, a proof of these clauses will be given below. Clauses (2), (6), (7) and (A2) are von Wright's four laws for the dissolution of deontic operators, while clauses (1), (5), (8)-(10) are some of the "laws on commitment." All these laws are mentioned in von Wright's article, "Deontic Logic." They are listed here for their historic interest. Therefore, only clauses (1)-(4) will be proved.

Proof:

(1) ⊢ [(A→B)∧A]→B by propositional logic. Therefore, by (DR1), ⊢ O[(A→B)∧A]→OB. By (A2) and propositional logic, we deduce that ⊢ [O(A→B)∧OA]→OB. This yields by propositional logic that ⊢ O(A→B)→(OA→OB). Q.E.D.

(2) ⊢ A→(A∨B) by propositional logic. By (DR1) we get ⊢ OA→O(A∨B). Similarly, since ⊢ B→(A∨B) by propositional logic, we also get ⊢ OB→O(A∨B) by (DR1). Hence, it follows by propositional logic that ⊢ (OA∨OB)→O(A∨B). Q.E.D.

(3) (A1) states that ⊢ ~(OA∧O~A). Therefore, by (A2), ⊢ ~O(A∧~A).

(4) (A1) states that ⊢ ~(OA∧O~A). Therefore, by propositional logic ⊢ OA→~O~A. By definition (b') of P, ⊢ OA→PA. Q.E.D.

This then is our standard system for deontic logic. But often when deontic logicians refer to SDL they include another axiom not proposed by von Wright:[10]

(A3) O(A∨~A).

Hansson claims that "even if von Wright did not propose [(A3)], it seems fair to define SDL as the logic which has [(A1)]-[(A3)] as axioms and the language described [earlier], and still claim that SDL is essentially what von Wright meant."[11] But as a matter of fact, it is not fair to claim that (A1)-(A3) is essentially what von Wright meant. In "Deontic Logic," von Wright argues explicitly against introducing (A3) as an axiom to his system.[12]

In the next section, we argue in support of

13

von Wright's position on (A3). Also, in the rest of
this work SDL⁻ refers only to axioms (A1) and (A2)
together with (R1), (R2), (R3') and (R4). SDL refers
only to SDL⁻ together with (A3). Following von
Wright's lead, we refer to his two systems solely as
"the Old System" and "the New System". We shall argue
that the principles underlying SDL⁻ are defensible,
but we do not intend to argue that the principle
underlying (A3) is.

2. Some Arguments for Rejecting (A3).

Several deontic logicians have espoused (A3) as
an axiom. Their reasons for such an espousal are not
adequate. In "The Logic of Conditional Obligation,"
van Fraassen presents his system of conditional
obligation. The system includes a rule of inference
which entails an axiom corresponding to (A3) in that
system. As he states himself, van Fraassen introduces
this rule because it enables him to derive a specific
desirable result within his system.[13] No more is said
in the article in defense of this rule. Therefore,
one can conclude that its introduction to van Fraassen's
system was based solely on pragmatic grounds.
Segerberg introduces the rule-version of (A3) to his
system without any discussion, while Hansson advocates
its introduction for two reasons.[14] a) Its usefulness.
Here, Hansson introduces two alternative bases for
SDL. The two bases become equivalent with the
addition of (A3). So Hansson suggests that (A3) be
admitted as part of the SDL base. b) The content of
(A3) is very small.

We shall not argue that an axiom may not be
introduced into a deontic system on the basis of its
usefulness. On the contrary, we agree on that matter
with A. N. Prior's comment on axiom (A3') which is a
stronger version of (A3), and which states that "if
it is necessary that A, then it ought to be the case
that A," i.e., $\vdash \Box A \rightarrow OA$ where $\Box$ is read as "it is
necessary that." He says:

> But surely this proposition is
> harmless (this obligation, if it
> be one, is one that is always

met, and need not worry us);
and better than fussing about its
oddity would be to use this result
to simplify our postulates.[15]

But usefulness is not usually the sole criterion for choosing axioms for a system. In formulating a system we are as well concerned with capturing some of the basic intuitions involve. It is owing to this fact that the deontic analogue to the alethic modal principle: "if it is necessary that A, then A is the case," while convenient in many ways, was dropped. Our intuitions with respect to (A3) are not as clear, but they do cast some doubts on the axioms. In the same article from which we quoted above, Prior refers to axiom (A3'), as a "paradox."[16] Føllesdal and Hilpinen remark that "the denial of [(A3)] seems fairly innocuous from the intuitive point of view" and point out that several logicians have rejected (A3).[17]

Therefore, while the content of (A3) might be small as Hansson argued, nevertheless, it appears from the statements above to be interesting enough not to go unnoticed. In effect (A3) guarantees that obligations always exist, no matter what situation is being considered. But there is no foundation in our deontic intuitions for such an assumption. On the contrary, if one holds, say, that the notion of obligation presupposes the emergence of a social structure, then the assumption that obligations always exist becomes false in that instance. Thus a clarification of the notion of obligation and its presuppositions could contribute to the clarification of our intuitions on (A3). Another disturbing feature of (A3) is the following: (A3) may be read: "It ought to be the case that (A∨∼A) is true." Deontic logicians agree that the primary notion of obligation being treated in their systems is that of moral obligation. Now one can argue that our logical laws are necessary. But there is no basis for arguing that there is a moral obligation for these laws to be true.

But there are no conclusive logical arguments for or against (A3). Ultimately, the argument for or against (A3) rests on our vague intuitions. We remark this quotation from von Wright:

> Ordinary language and our common sense logical intuitions seem not to provide us with any clear answer. It appears, moreover, that no further considerations can help us to decide on the issue. It may be thought 'awkward' to permit contradictory actions but it is difficult to conceive of any logical argument against this permission. From the point of view of logic, therefore, the most plausible course seems to be to regard $P(A \wedge \sim A)$ and $O(A \vee \sim A)$ as expressing contingent propositions which can be either true or false.[18]

In Chapter IV, it will become clear that an acceptable standard deontic logic can be formulated without (A3). For this reason, we shall restrict our definition of SDL to von Wright's original system and consequently formulate a standard system based on SDL$^-$. (A3) or its denial can then be considered as expressing contingent propositions which can be either true or false.

3. Some Arguments in Favor of the Basic Principles of SDL$^-$.

   a. The Principle that Consequences of what Ought to be the Case Ought to be the Case. We are now left with two axioms and four inference rules as the object of our study. Of these four rules, (R3) stands out as especially interesting since together with (A2) it yields, as we showed in Section 1, (DR1). (DR1) expresses in SDL$^-$ the widely accepted principle.

P. Consequences of what ought to be the case ought to be the case.

(DR1) is highly intuitive and the principle it expresses is a basic principle of our deontic reasoning. We use it daily in our deliberations. For example, when we are told that it ought to be the case that we obey our parents, we conclude correctly and by virtue of P that it ought to be the case that we obey our mothers. Similarly, if it ought to be the case that we sing and dance at a friend's party, then it certainly ought to be the case that we sing at that party. Thus, principle P is not only intuitive but it permeates our most basic moral reasoning.

It is worth noting at this point that several philosophers have chosen the following principle as the formal counterpart to P:

(NP) $(A \Rightarrow B) \rightarrow (OA \Rightarrow OB)$

where "$\Rightarrow$" is read as "necessarily implies." This formulation appears mostly in deontic systems using the Anderson Simplification.[19] The Anderson Simplification is obtained by taking as a primitive deontic concept a constant S, read as "the sanction." Forbiddance and obligation are then defined in terms of S in the following manner: "A is forbidden" means "A necessitates the sanction," i.e., $A \Rightarrow S$; "A is obligatory" means "~A necessitates the sanction," i.e., $\sim A \Rightarrow S$.[20]

We shall not discuss here Anderson's Simplification and its shortcomings. We simply refer the reader to our work "A Critical Survey in Deontic Logic" where Anderson's Simplification is discussed and criticized in detail.[21] Similar discussions have been presented by Nowell-Smith and Lemmon, as well as Powers.[22]

We also note that the principle (NP) yields in modal system T or any stronger modal system, our SDL⁻ rule (DR1).[23] In later sections, we shall make use of the literature involving (NP).[24] As it turns out, many of the contributions made there can be restated in terms of (DR1).

Finally, we note that in deontic systems containing the unary operator F for "it is forbidden that..." a principle similar to P, which we name P', is also asserted.[25] It states that "whatever implies what is forbidden is itself forbidden." Formally,

(FR) $\dfrac{\vdash A \to B}{\vdash FB \to FA}$

An example of a situation where this principle would be applied can be easily given. From the fact that it is forbidden for someone to sing in public, it follows by P' that it is forbidden for this person to sing and dance in public. This example reveals that like principle P, P' is also a plausible and widely accepted principle. Logicians using the Anderson Simplification introduced a counterpart to this principle too, in the manner discussed above with respect to P.

    b. The Principle that Ought-Statements do not Conflict. Another major deontic principle asserted by SDL⁻ is that ought-statements do not conflict. This is expressed by (A1), and the literature is replete with arguments in defense of this principle. We shall mention here two such arguments. First, it is pointed out that moral principles which license ought-statements belong to some sort of an ethical hierarchy. Hence, when two ought-statements seem to conflict, the issue can be easily resolved by referring to the principle licensing each ought-statement and its position in the hierarchy. The ought-statement backed by the highest principle overrides the other.[26] Second, it is pointed out that given the common principle that "what is obligatory is permitted," one can derive logically the principle that ought-statements do not conflict.[27] Formally, the derivation proceeds as follows:

$OA \to PA$.

$OA \to \sim O\sim A$ by definition of P.

∴ $\sim[OA \wedge O\sim A]$ by propositional logic.

    Hence, like (DR1) and (FR), (A1) is highly intuitive and plausible.

    c. The Principle that "Ought" Implies "Can".

One more principle asserted in SDL⁻ deserves some discussion. It is expressed by (A2) which is the conjunction of two statements:

(A2.1) $O(A \wedge B) \rightarrow (OA \wedge OB)$.

(A2.2) $(OA \wedge OB) \rightarrow O(A \wedge B)$.

Let us consider (A2.1) first. (A2.1) is an intuitive principle. Certainly if it ought to be the case that one sings and dances at a friend's party, then it follows that it ought to be the case that one sings at that party. It is this part of (A2) which allowed us to derive (DR1) in Section II.1.

But this intuitive principle yields, when combined with (A1), the assertion that "it is false that the impossible ought to be the case." Others have stated this result as "no one is under an obligation to do the impossible."[28] It is usually referred to as the Kantian principle, or the principle that "ought" implies "can".[29] Formally, it can be stated as: $\sim O(A \wedge \sim A)$.

In introducing this Kantian principle to his system, Prior found it sufficient to remark that "it will be generally regarded as reasonable."[30] Many examples come to mind as illustrations of the reasonableness of the principle that "ought" implies "can". If a young man is an invalid, then it is false that it ought to be the case that he joins the army in defense of his country, even if young men are required to do so. Similarly, while it ought to be the case that dutiful children visit their elderly parents regularly, a dutiful child who is in jail is not under that obligation. The legal code, which is akin to the moral code, also gives credence to the principle "ought" implies "can". A citizen is not punished for acts that were impossible for him to avoid. This principle, therefore, coincides with our common sense intuitions.

We now turn our attention to (A2.2). Again a preliminary look at this principle convinces us of its intuitiveness. After all, if it ought to be the case that one sings at a friend's party, and it ought to be the case that one dances at that party, then it clearly follows that one ought to sing and dance at that party.

But as Chellas points out, if we accept the Kantian principle which we argued for above, then on the basis of (A2.2) the Kantian principle yields the principle that obligations do not conflict.[31] "Since it is not obvious that no ethical theory can accept the possibility of genuine conflict of duties,"[32] Chellas goes on to reject (A2.2) "in order that the standpoint adopted [in his paper] be minimal."[33]

Earlier in this chapter, the principle that obligations do not conflict was briefly defended as a basic deontic principle. Later in this work its defense will be more thorough and detailed. Therefore, it is clear that in this work the fact that (A2.2) yields the principle that obligations do not conflict will not be regarded as an argument against the acceptance of (A2.2).

Van Fraassen also rejects (A2.2). He argues that since ethical conflict are possible, we may assert sometimes both OA and O∼A. Furthermore, "when we have arrived at two conclusions we can conjoin them:

$OA \land O{\sim}A$

can be true. But "ought" implies "can"...; so

$O(A \land {\sim}A)$

cannot be true."[34]

Again, clearly van Fraassen's reasons for rejecting (A2.2) are not compelling from our point of view since we do not hold the view that ethical conflicts are possible. Consequently, we cannot correctly assert OA and O∼A at the same time. The intuitiveness of (A2.2) is thus preserved.

4. An Explication of the Notion of "Paradox" as Used in Deontic Logic.

We have argued in Section 3 in support of the major principles underlying SDL⁻. Several examples were presented to illustrate their intuitiveness. But as we mentioned in the Introduction, those principles have generated several paradoxes in deontic logic. Thus their plausibility has been questioned by many philosophers, and a trend appeared in which some or all of these principles were rejected.

Before embarking on an exposition of these paradoxes, it is necessary to discuss first what deontic logicians meant by calling them paradoxes. Except in rare cases none of these paradoxes was developed in such a way as to reveal a logical contradiction. Hence, these are not paradoxes in this strong sense. A survey of the literature reveals that they have been referred to alternatively as puzzles or dilemmas.[35] This is a good clue as to the nature of the notion involved here.

An accurate explication of the notion of "paradox" as used in deontic logic was given by Nowell-Smith and Lemmon in their article "Escapism: The Logical Basis of Ethics." In discussing principle P', introduced here in Section 3.2, and the paradox related to it, they say that:

> This is not a logician's paradox, like Russell's class paradox; it reveals no logical antinomy or contradiction within the calculus. It is simply that [P']... gives when interpreted, a result which is not only surprising, but unpalatable.[36]

Hansson concurs with Nowell-Smith and Lemmon. He remarks that

> Some theorems of SDL have been called paradoxes. This means, of course, that they seem counter-intuitive, although they are derived from intuitively acceptable axioms.[37]

In his article, "The Paradoxes of Derived Obligation,"

Prior points out that some paradoxes of deontic logic are deontic analogues of the paradoxes of strict implication.[38]

Thus, in their discussion and use of this notion deontic logicians agree with Quine's explication given in his article, "The Ways of Paradox." There Quine reserves the special term "antinomy" for paradoxes which "produce a self-contradiction by accepted ways of reasoning." But he supplies a general definition of paradox as "just any conclusion that at first sounds absurd but that has an argument to sustain it."[39] Thus, the notion of "paradox" as used by deontic logicians has a foundation in the general literature on logic.

5. The Paradoxes of Deontic Logic.

We are now in a position to introduce the paradoxes of deontic logic.

a. Ross' Paradox.[40] This paradox rests on the following statement which is derivable in SDL⁻ from (DR1) as we demonstrated in Section 1:

$\vdash (OA \vee OB) \rightarrow O(A \vee B)$

Hence, it is a paradox that involves principle P. It proceeds as follows:

1. It ought to be the case that Arthur helps Jones.

Now, let A stand for: Arthur helps Jones.
And, let B stand for: Arthur kills Jones.

We now have the following argument:

(1')   OA.
∴(2') OA∨OB   by (1') and rules of propositional logic.
∴(3') O(A∨B) by (2') and the theorem above.

In English (3') reads as:

(3) It ought to be the case that either Arthur helps Jones or he kills him.

Clearly, the obligation expressed by (3) is satisfiable by killing Jones, which is absurd.

  b. Åqvist's Paradox.[41] This paradox involves principle P introduced in Section 3.a and which is expressed in SDL⁻ by (DR1).

  An intuitively consistent set of sentences is introduced:

(1) It ought to be that Smith refrains from robbing Jones.
(2) It ought to be that the Samaritan helps Jones, whom Smith robs (has robbed).

These two sentences are then formalized according to the following scheme:

A: Smith robs Jones.
B: The Samaritan helps Jones.

We then get:

(1') $O \sim A$.
(2') $O(A \wedge B)$.

Åqvist then argues that by propositional calculus and (DR1) we can derive OA from (2'), i.e., that it ought to be the case that Smith robs Jones.[42] The result is not only counter-intuitive, but in a system that accepts the principle that obligations do not conflict, discussed in Section 3.b, it yields together with (1') a formal contradiction.

  c. The Good Samaritan Paradox.[43] This paradox involves principle P′ introduced with P in Section II:3.a. It is based on the following two premises:

(1) If the Good Samaritan helps Jones who was robbed, then Jones was robbed.

(2) It is forbidden that Jones be robbed.

Let A stand for: The Good Samaritan helps Jones.
Let B stand for: Jones was robbed.

The paradox can now be derived in this manner:

(1') $(A \wedge B) \rightarrow B$.
(2') FB.

Therefore, by (FR), we can conclude that:

(3') $F(A \wedge B)$.

That is,

(3) It is forbidden that the Good Samaritan helps Jones who was robbed.

which is absurd.

    d. The Robber's Paradox.[44] This paradox also involves principle P. We point out that:

(1) The robber repenting his robbery implies that robbery has occurred.
(2) It is forbidden that robbery occur.

By reasoning similar to that used in the Good Samaritan Paradox, we conclude that:

(3) It is forbidden that the robber repents his robbery.

    e. The Victim's Paradox.[45] Also involving principle P, this paradox states that since

(1) If the victim of robbery bemoans his fate of being robbed, then a robbery has occurred.

and since,

(2) It is forbidden that robbery occurs,

then

(3) It is forbidden that the victim of robbery bemoans his fate of being robbed.

    f. Plato's Paradox.[46] This paradox involves the

principle that obligations do not conflict. The principle is expressed in SDL⁻ by (A1), and was discussed in Section 3.b. The specific version of this paradox which will be presented below is due to E. J. Lemmon:

> A friend leaves me with his gun, saying that he will be back for it in the evening, and I promise to return it when he calls. He arrives in a distraught condition, demands his gun and announces that he is going to shoot his wife because she has been unfaithful. I ought to return the gun, since I promised to do so--a case of obligation. And yet I ought not to do so, since to do so would be to be indirectly responsible for a murder, and my moral principles are such that I regard this as wrong.[47]

   g. Sartre's Paradox. This paradox constructed by Sartre was also used by deontic logic to attack the deontic principle expressed in SDL⁻ by (A1).[48] This paradox is similar to Plato's paradox. But Lemmon distinguishes them by remarking that Plato's paradox belongs to the class of cases where a person both ought and ought not to do something, while Sartre's paradox belongs to the class of cases where there is some but not conclusive evidence that one ought to do something, and there is some but not conclusive evidence that one ought not to do that thing.[49]

   Sartre's paradox concerns a pupil of his who had lost his brother in the war against Germany and wanted to avenge him by joining the Free French Forces. This young man also had a mother who was deeply wounded by the death of her oldest son and became deeply attached to this son. The crux of the paradox is that there is a good but not conclusive argument to the effect that Sartre's pupil ought to stay by his mother's side. Similarly, there is a good but not conclusive argument to the effect that he ought to join the Free French Forces. However, the latter ought-statement conflicts with the first, so that, when expressed formally in a standard deontic system, the two ought-statements contradict (A1).

h. The Paradox of the Contrary-to-Duty Imperative.[50] A deontic logician who accepts (A1) and the following two facts:

(i) that we neglect our duties occasionally, and
(ii) that one must make the best of a bad situation resulting from (i),

will find this paradox especially challenging.[51] One version proceeds as follows:

(1) Jones robs Smith.
(2) Jones ought not to rob Smith.
(3) It ought to be that if Jones doesn't rob Smith, he is not punished.
(4) If Jones robs Smith, then he ought to be punished.

(4) is what Chisholm calls a contrary-do-duty imperative, i.e., an imperative which tells us what we ought to do if we neglect certain duties.[52]

Mott notes three adequacy conditions pertaining to any symbolic representation of (1)-(4).[53]

(a.1) The representation be consistent.
(a.2) The entailment between (1) and (4) and "Jones ought to be punished" be preserved.
(a.3) The representation of "it ought to be that if Jones does not rob Smith then he is punished" is false.

Given these criteria, the problem centers around representing (3) and (4) in SDL^-. (3) cannot be represented as $(\sim A \rightarrow O \sim B)$, because for consistency the statement "It ought to be that if Jones does not rob Smith he is punished" must then be represented as $(\sim A \rightarrow OB)$ which is true contrary to (a.3) by virtue of (1). Furthermore, (4) cannot be represented as $O(A \rightarrow B)$ because then (a.2) is violated; OB is not a consequence of A and $O(A \rightarrow B)$ in any standard deontic logic.

There is also another argument for rejecting the

representation of $O(A \rightarrow B)$. We know from logic that:

$\vdash \sim A \rightarrow (\sim A \vee B)$, for any B

and

$\vdash (\sim A \vee B) \leftrightarrow (A \rightarrow B)$.

So by principle P, we can conclude that:

$\vdash O \sim A \rightarrow O(A \rightarrow B)$, for any B.

That is, if it ought not to be the case that A, then no matter what B is we can affirm that it is obligatory that if A then B.

That this result is unacceptable is shown by the following argument of Chisholm's:

> Let us suppose we wish to remind a potential thief of the duty to restore stolen property. The locution of the obligatory conditional--'It is obligatory that if you steal then you return the money'-- is not adequate for what we want to say. For, if stealing is wrong, then this locution 'O (if A then B)', interpreted [in the way described above], also allows us to say, "It is obligatory that if you steal then you do not return the money' and indeed, 'It is obligatory that if you steal then you steal again and lead a life of sin henceforth.[54]

Hence, (3) and (4) must be represented differently in SDL^-. The other possibility is to represent (3) as $O(\sim A \rightarrow \sim B)$ and to represent (4) as $(A \rightarrow OB)$. But this will not do either, since (1) and (4) now yield:

(5) It ought to be the case that Jones is punished.

while (2) and (3) yield by clause (1) of theorem T_0:

(6) It ought to be the case that Jones is not punished.

The conjunction of (4) and (6) contradicts (A1).

Both alternatives for representing an ought-statement have failed for both (3) and (4). This is the crux of the paradox. We need to find an adequate way for representing (3) and (4) in SDL⁻.

i. The Epistemic Obligation Paradox.[55] This paradox arises within an extension of SDL⁻ which includes the operator K read as 'I know that...', and the following theorem valid in epistemic logic:

⊢ KA→A.

We now consider this intuitively consistent set:

(1) It ought to be that Smith refrains from robbing Jones.

and

(2) I ought to know that Smith robs Jones.

We can formalize the set above as follows:

Let A stand for: Smith robs Jones.

(1') O∼A
(2') OKA

By the epistemic theorem mentioned above, and (DR1),

(2') yields:
(3') OA

which together with (1') is inconsistent with (A1).

The nine paradoxes above are the best known paradoxes in the literature. The first eight have been central in the on-going debate concerning the validity of the principles of SDL⁻. Therefore, since our claim is that the principles of SDL⁻ are essentially correct, it becomes necessary for us to dispose of this multitude of paradoxes.

6. Sorting the Paradoxes of Deontic Logic into Three Main Groups.

The task of disposing of all these paradoxes looks tiresomely long, but not if we observe a few crucial facts about them. First, in most deontic systems that include the unary operator F, F is defined as O∼.[56] (A notable exception in this case is Hintikka's system. His argument for the rejection of F=O∼ has been criticized elsewhere.[57]) Under the common definition, principle P turns out to be equivalent to principle P'.[58] As a result, the Åqvist paradox and the Good Samaritan paradox turn out to be two versions of the same paradox. Furthermore, the Robber's Paradox and the Victim's Paradox are special cases of the Good Samaritan Paradox that were introduced to discredit inadequate solutions that appeared in the literature.[59] Therefore, while keeping in mind all the various versions, we need concentrate on one only. Åqvist's version is the O-version of the original Good Samaritan paradox which we described in 4c. Since the system we are dealing with takes O as a deontic primitive and defines F as O∼, we shall choose Åqvist's version to represent this host of paradoxes.

Historically, the Good Samaritan paradox was presented in the form described in c. Thus, the original version of this paradox was the F version. But since then and in light of the definition of F, philosophers have used the same name to refer to the O-version of the paradox.[60] Åqvist himself describes his paradox as a version of the Good Samaritan paradox.[61] Therefore, in light of the definition of F as O∼ and its resulting effect on the paradoxes listed under 4b and 4c, and in light of a more recent trend in the literature we shall refer to the paradox introduced in 4b, and which we referred to then as Åqvist's paradox, as the Good Samaritan paradox. Our treatment of this paradox in Chapter III will succeed in resolving as well the other versions discussed in 4c, 4d and 4e.

Secondly, the next two paradoxes, Plato's paradox and Sartre's paradox shall be referred to by the same general name, "the Conflict-of-Duty paradox." One reason behind giving them this common name is that in discussing conflict of duties, philosophers did not usually distinguish between the two cases.[62] Another reason is that both paradoxes question the principle that ought-statements do not conflict. As a result the resolution of both paradoxes is highly similar. This fact will become clear in Chapter III where both paradoxes are treated and resolved together.

Thirdly, since we shall argue in defense of SDL^-, the Contrary-to-Duty Imperative paradox represents a serious challenge to our position. The paradox will be discussed at length and resolved in Chapter IV.

Thus, the first eight paradoxes can be grouped in three main groups:

    I.   Paradoxes involving the principle P.
         These are of two kinds:

         a. Ross' paradox.
         b. The Good Samaritan paradox.

    II. Paradoxes involving (A1).

         a. Plato's paradox.
         b. Sartre's paradox.

         Both a and b are referred to in the literature as the Conflict-of-Duty paradox.

    III. The Paradox of the Contrary-to-Duty Imperative.

         The solution to this paradox depends on the solution we give to paradoxes in group II. Therefore, we should concentrate first on the first two groups of deontic paradoxes.

As for the ninth paradox, called the paradox of Epistemic Obligation, though it is a well-known paradox, it has not played a crucial role in the development of deontic logic. We do not think that this paradox deserves attention in a discussion on deontic logic because the common locution involved in its formulation "ought to know" is not correctly represented by OK. To illustrate this, consider the following example:

You have a headache.

Then,

You ought to know you have a headache.

Let A stand for: "You have a headache."

(1)   A→OKA.

But

(2)   OKA→OA

by (DR1) and the theorem mentioned in Section 5.i. Hence,

(3)   A→OA.

That is, if you have a headache, it ought to be the case that you have it.[63] Therefore, the paradox of Epistemic Obligation seems to lead us into a discussion of adequate ways for formalizing the notion "ought to know" which is not a notion proper to deontic logic. It is therefore beyond the scope of this study and will not be treated here.

7. The General Lines for Resolving the Paradoxes.

In Section 4, we explained the notion of "paradox" as used in the literature on deontic logic. The notion it turns out is much weaker than that used sometimes in set theory. Therefore, we must investigate what is meant in a "resolution" of the paradoxes in this context.

Having defined this weak notion of "paradox" in deontic logic, Hansson adds that "The general line of a 'solution' is then to point out that the concepts involved are ambiguous."[64] This general line of a solution describes correctly our approach and resolution of the Good Samaritan paradox, and the Conflict-of-Duty Paradox. But it does not describe accurately other method by which the other paradoxes were resolved. Ross' Paradox will be resolved in Chapter III by showing that it appears as paradoxical only because some of its premises are not stated explicitly in the argument. While in treating the paradox of the Contrary-to-Duty Imperative in Chapter IV the proposed solution requires the introduction of a new notion into our deontic system; that of a dyadic operator $O(/)$. In short, the resolution of the paradoxes will be varied in accordance with the nature of each paradox.

Footnotes

Chapter II

[1] The "Old System of Deontic Logic" is the way Georg Henrik von Wright refers to the system he proposed in his article "Deontic Logic," Mind 60 (1951), 1-15. The reference is made in von Wright's article "A New System of Deontic Logic," <u>Deontic Logic: Introductory and Systematic Readings</u>, ed. Risto Hilpinen (New York: Humanities Press 1971), 105.

[2] Dagfinn Føllesdal and Risto Hilpinen, "Deontic Logic: An Introduction," Hilpinen, 13.

[3] von Wright, "Deontic Logic," 3.

[4] See for example Bengt Hansson, "An Analysis of Some Deontic Logics," Hilpinen, 121-148.

[5] von Wright, "Deontic Logic," 3. Hintikka represents an exception to this consensus. His position is evaluated (reference to article as in footnote 57).

[6] von Wright, "A New System", 105.

[7] See for example Bas van Fraassen, "The Logic of Conditional Obligation," <u>Journal of Philosophy</u> 1 (1972), 426. Also, Jaakko Hintikka, "Some Main Problems of Deontic Logic," Hilpinen, 60. Also, E. J. Lemmon, "Deontic Logic and the Logic of Imperatives," <u>Logique et Analyse,</u> n.s., 29 (1965), 39.

[8] von Wright, "A New System," 106.

[9] von Wright, "Deontic Logic," passim.

[10] See for example Føllesdal and Hilpinen, 13.

[11] Hansson, 128.

[12] von Wright, "Deontic Logic," 11.

[13] van Fraassen, "Conditional Obligation," 421.

[14] Krister Segerberg, "Some Logics of Commitment and Obligation," Hilpinen, 152. Hansson, p. 128.

[15] A. N. Prior, "Escapism: The Logical Basis of Ethics," *Essays in Moral Philosophy*, ed. A. I. Melden, (Seattle: University of Washington Press, 1958), 138.

[16] Ibid., 141.

[17] Føllesdal and Hilpinen, 13.

[18] von Wright, "Deontic Logic," 10-11. The symbol for conjunction has been changed in this quotation. Similarly, other quotations in this work will be changed to make them consistent with the notation used here.

[19] See for example Prior. Also P. H. Nowell-Smith and E. J. Lemmon, "Escapism: The Logical Basis of Ethics," Mind 69 (1960), 289-300.

[20] Prior, 138.

[21] Azizah al-Hibri Cox, "A Critical Survey in Deontic Logic," Master's thesis, (Detroit: Wayne State University, 1968), 14-20.

[22] Nowell-Smith and Lemmon, 296-300. Also, Lawrence Powers, "Some Deontic Logicians," *Nous* 4 (1967), 397-9.

[23] The proof is simple. Assume NP, i.e. $(A \rightarrow B) \rightarrow (OA \rightarrow OB)$. Strict implication $\rightarrow$ is defined by Anderson as follows: $(A \rightarrow B) = \Box(A \to B)$ in his article "Some Nasty Problems in the Formal Logic of Ethics," *Nous* 1 (1967), 353. Therefore, (NP) can be restated as: $\Box(A \to B) \to \Box(OA \to OB)$. Suppose that $\vdash A \to B$. By any modal logic of at least strength T, we get,

$\vdash \Box(A \rightarrow B)$
$\therefore \vdash \Box(OA \rightarrow OB)$ by (NP)
$\therefore \vdash (OA \rightarrow OB)$ by the axioms of any such modal logic.

For a discussion of modal system T and other modal systems see G. E. Hughes and M. J. Cresswell, <u>An Introduction to Modal Logic</u>, (London: Methuen & Co., 1973), es. 31.

[24] See for example our discussion of the proposed solutions to the Good Samaritan Paradox in Chapter III.

[25] See for example Prior, 144.

[26] Hector-Neri Castañeda, "A Theory of Morality," <u>Philosophy and Phenomenological Research</u> 17 (1957), 344.

[27] van Fraassen, "Values and the Heart's Command," <u>Journal of Philosophy</u> 70 (1973), 12.

[28] Ibid.

[29] Ibid., 15.

[30] Prior, 138.

[31] Brian F. Chellas, "Conditional Obligation," <u>Logical Theory and Semantic Analysis: Essays Dedicated to Stig Kanger on his Fiftieth Birthday</u>, ed. Soren Stenlund (Dordrecht: D. Reidel Publishing Co., 1974), 24.

[32] Ibid., 24.

[33] Ibid.

[34] van Fraassen, "Values," 15.

[35] See for example Lennart Åqvist, "Good Samaritans, Contrary-to-Duty Imperatives and Epistemic Obligations," <u>Nous</u> 1 (1967), 362. Also, see Lemmon, "Moral Dilemmas," <u>Philosophical Review</u> 71 (1962), passim.

[36] Nowell-Smith and Lemmon, 290.

[37] Hansson, p. 130.

[38] Prior, "The Paradoxes of Derived Obligation," Mind 63 (1954), 64.

[39] W. V. Quine, "The Ways of Paradox," <u>The Ways of Paradox and Other Essays</u>, (New York: Random House, 1966), 3. See also 7.

[40] Alf Ross, "Imperatives and Logic," *Theoria* 7 (1941), 53-71.

[41] Åqvist, 366.

[42] Ibid., 366.

[43] Prior, "Escapism," 144.

[44] Nowell-Smith and Lemmon, 294.

[45] Ibid., 293.

[46] The attribution of this paradox to Plato was suggested by Lemmon in "Moral Dilemmas," 152.

[47] Ibid., 148.

[48] van Fraassen, "Values", 10.

[49] Ibid., 152.

[50] This specific version is borrowed from Peter L. Mott, "On Chisholm's Paradox," *Journal of Philosophical Logic* 2 (1973), 197.

[51] These two facts were stated by Roderick Chisholm in the introduction to his article, "Contrary-to-Duty Imperatives and Deontic Logic," *Analysis* 24 (1963), 33.

[52] Ibid., 33.

[53] Mott, 196-197.

[54] Chisholm, 34.

[55] Åqvist, 366.

[56] See, for example, von Wright, "Deontic Logic," 3.

[57] See my article, "Hintikka and the Interdefinability of Obligation and Forbiddance," *Southwestern Journal of Philosophy*, forthcoming.

[58] Let us show that the formal counterparts of P and P , i.e., (DR1) and (FR) respectively are equivalent. (DR1) states that

$$\frac{\vdash A \to B}{\vdash OA \to OB}$$

But $\vdash A \to B$ means that $\vdash {\sim}B \to {\sim}A$. Hence, by (DR1), we get:

$$\frac{\vdash A \rightarrow B}{\vdash O{\sim}B \rightarrow O{\sim}A}$$

which is the same as:

$$\frac{\vdash A \rightarrow B}{\vdash FB \rightarrow FA}$$

The reverse, namely, the derivation of (DR1) from (FR) is just as obvious.

[59] See Nowell-Smith and Lemmon, 293-294.

[60] See for example van Fraassen, "Conditional Obligation," 424.

[61] Åqvist, 366.

[62] See for example van Fraassen, "Values," 8-11.

[63] I am debted to Brian Chellas for drawing my attention to the unusual consequences of expressing "you ought to know that A" as OKA.

[64] Hansson, 131.

CHAPTER III

RESOLUTIONS OF THE FIRST TWO GROUPS OF DEONTIC PARADOXES

A. A Resolution of the First Group of Paradoxes of Deontic Logic

1. On the Relation between (DR1) and Ross' Paradox.

This paradox is also known as the paradox of Disjunctive Obligation. As was shown in Section II:5.a it is based on theorem T_0 of SDL$^-$. In Section II:1 theorem T_0 was derived from (DR1). We now establish that the relation between theorem T_0 and (DR1) is even stronger.

Theorem.

In any deontic system containing propositional logic and (R3'), if

(D) $\vdash$ (OA$\vee$OB)$\rightarrow$O(A$\vee$B).

Then we can derive from (D) together with (R3') only, the rule (DR1).

To prove the theorem we assume that $\vdash$ A$\rightarrow$B and derive $\vdash$ OA$\rightarrow$OB. By our assumption and propositional logic,

$\vdash$ (A$\vee$B)$\leftrightarrow$B.

Consequently, we assert by (R3') that

$\vdash$ O(A$\vee$B)$\leftrightarrow$OB

which yields by (D), that

$\vdash$ (OA$\vee$OB)$\rightarrow$OB

i.e., $\vdash$ OA$\rightarrow$OB. Q.E.D.

Thus, by the theorem we just proved and the result established in Section II:1 concerning (D), we can conclude that a system containing (D), (R3') and propositional logic is equivalent to one containing (DR1), (R3') and propositional logic. In such systems then (D) can be regarded as an axiomatic form of the rule (DR1). Similarly, it can be shown that (D) is equivalent to (A2.1) in SDL$^-$. In Section II:1 it was (A2.1) together with (R3') that allowed us to derive (DR1).[1] The significance of Ross' paradox is clearly enhanced by these results.

2. Beatty's Argument against one Version of (DR1).

Several attempts have been made to dismiss this paradox by arguing that there is nothing paradoxical about (3'),[2] O(A∨B), but Beatty holds a different position. In his article, "On Evaluating Deontic Logics," Beatty discusses a version of Ross' paradox which involves the notion of conditional obligation.[3] Consequently, the paradox is discussed in light of a version of (DR1) which involves the same notion. We need not concern ourselves at this stage with these complications. Therefore, we shall reconstruct Beatty's argument (and quotations) so as to delete the notion of conditional obligation in favor of the old unconditional notion. We must note though that the thrust of Beatty's argument remains unchanged after the reconstruction. Furthermore, one can easily verify that the thrust of our criticism of Beatty also remains unchanged when the original version is considered.

Beatty observes correctly that,

> [(DR1)] clearly licenses the inference of [O(A∨B)] from [OA]. Now the following situation might be one in which a sentence of the form [OA] is true while [O(A∨B)] is false.[4]

He then proceeds to provide an example of disjunctive obligation, which is a variant of Ross' paradox. He remarks that (using our example of Section II:5.a), (3'), i.e., O(A∨B) carries the suggestion that Arthur can discharge his obligation by satisfying OA where OB stands for "It ought to be the case that Arthur

kills Jones." Hence, while accepting (1') he rejects
(3') which is a consequence of (1') by (DR1) as false,
although he admits that "it is difficult to account in
any precise way for the intuition that [(3')] is not
true in the situation under consideration."[5] His case
against (DR1) rests on intuitions that are difficult
to substantiate.

   Beatty then makes a further attempt to reveal the
implausibility of (DR1) and backs his intuitions with
some explanations: He suggests that we construe
obligation sentences in the following manner: A in OA
is a description of an action. He then states that
while OA above describes the action correctly, (3')
misdescribes it. Therefore,

> This new construal of sentence letters
> and formulas, however, places the rule
> [(DR1)] in a somewhat different perspec-
> tive... now it can be viewed as saying
> that you can correctly be described as
> obligated to do... all the logical
> consequences of what you can correctly
> be described as obligated to do... .
> Put this way, in terms of description,
> the rule seems much less plausible.[6]

3. Response to Beatty.

   Beatty's claim that (1') (using our example of
Section II:5.a) describes Arthur's obligation correctly
while (3') misdescribes it, begs the point in question.
It only restates his earlier intuitions, related to
the usual reading of OA, on the same sentences; which
intuitions he found "difficult to account for."[7]
Therefore, recasting the whole problem in new terminology is of no help in this case. Similarly, his new
reading of (DR1) is no less plausible than saying that
"it is true that you have an obligation to do all the
logical consequences of what it is true that you have
an obligation to do," which is one old way of stating
(DR1).

   Beatty's claim that (DR1) as construed by him
appears as much less plausible, raises two questions:

a) Why should we accept this reading? b) Why is this reading much less plausible? Presumably, his answer to the first question is that his new construal of obligation sentences, which leads to this reading, helps to distinguish between "correctly described obligations" and "misdescribed obligations." This distinction, Beatty believes, is crucial for weeding out Ross' paradox. It exposes (DR1) as an implausible principle. This leads us to Beatty's answer of the second question. (DR1) is implausible because it claims that one can correctly be described as obligated to do all the logical consequences of what one can correctly be described as obligated to do. Yet, Beatty claims that he produced, by his example, a case where (DR1) led from correctly described obligations to misdescribed ones. This is the crux of Beatty's case against (DR1). But as we pointed out earlier, this whole argument begs the question by assuming from the beginning that (3') misdescribes the obligation.

4. Solution to Ross' Paradox.

The basic fact to observe about an obligation of form (3'), i.e., $O(A \vee B)$, is that, indeed, it can be satisfied either by bringing about A or by bringing about B. In that we agree with Beatty. But this fact does not lead us to deny the truth of (3'). On the contrary, it leads us to note that since "it is forbidden that Arthur kills Jones" according to moral laws, then it follows that (3') can only be satisfied by satisfying OA. Formally,

$[O(A \vee B) \wedge O \sim B] \rightarrow O[(A \vee B) \wedge \sim B]$ by (A2.2)

which reduces by the usual rules of logic and (R3') to OA.

Therefore, the simple fact to remember about disjunctive obligations is that they present us with the choice on how to fulfill our obligations. But at no time should we choose a way of fulfilling one obligation by violating another, if such course of action can be avoided. (The case where this cannot be avoided will be discussed in Chapter IV.) This fact is guaranteed by (A2.2).

Hansson concurs "that somebody asserts an obligation does not mean that he approves of every way of making the obligatory formula true." This leads him to a conclusion similar to ours, namely, that in satisfying certain obligations "we must look not only on the obligations uttered or asserted, but on the deontic system as a whole."[8]

Our solution, while sharing Beatty's uneasiness about some possible but unacceptable ways of satisfying (3'), points to the method for eliminating these ways without rejecting (DR1). This resolves Ross' paradox.

5. The Various Proposed Solutions to the Good Samaritan Paradox.

As we pointed out in Sections II:5 and II:6 this paradox involves directly principle P which is expressed in SDL⁻ by (DR1). Yet, while Beatty found a reason in Ross' paradox for rejecting this principle, curiously enough, none of the solutions proposed for the Good Samaritan paradox is based on a rejection of principle P.

For the reader who is unfamiliar with the history of this paradox, let us mention now very briefly and in chronological order some of the more salient proposals for resolving it.[9] These proposals and others have been discussed in detail and subsequently rejected in our work, "A Critical Survey in Deontic Logic."[10] Therefore, for understanding the limitations of each proposal mentioned below, the reader is asked to refer to our earlier work.

One solution to this paradox was proposed by Prior who calls it the "existentialist" solution. It suggests that each person should regard deontic logic as applying to those measures he must take to avoid bringing about a state of affairs forbidden to him.[11]

In presenting this solution Prior utilizes an "F"-version of the Good Samaritan paradox. His version is couched in terms of Anderson's Simplification and consequently is directed against (NP). But if we remember that "FA" is defined as "A $\longrightarrow$ S" (see Section

II:3.a) then we can restate Prior's version as well as his argument solely in terms of "FA" without any reference to "S". His solution is revealed then to be as relevant to (DR1) as it was to (NP).

Prior argues that given his solution which requires each person to work within his own deontic logic, the statement "it is forbidden that the Good Samaritan helps Jones" is not derivable in the Samaritan's deontic logic. This is due to the fact that the statement needed for its derivation "it is forbidden that Jones be robbed" does not concern the Samaritan. It enters his logic merely to help "set the stage on which the acts for which he is responsible take place."[12] Therefore, it does not yield a prohibition-statement that concerns him. In order to reveal the inadequacy of Prior's proposed solution, the Robber's paradox and the Victim's paradox were formulated.[13]

Another proposal also tied to the Anderson Simplification was made by Nowell-Smith and Lemmon. As with Prior's solution, this one can be easily applied to our version of the Good Samaritan paradox (introduced in Section II:5.c) which involves (DR1). It requires the introduction of (i) agents in deontic statements and (ii) a particular constant predicate "Sx" interpreted as "x ought to suffer the sanction."[14] It is a more sophisticated solution than that of Prior. But while it solves this paradox it creates other problems.[15]

A third proposal was made by Rickman and a fourth by Robison. These proposals require the specification of persons, times and places in a deontic statement.[16] In our work cited earlier, we explain why this solution also fails.[17] Åqvist proposes yet another method for resolving the paradox through the use of two different senses of obligation (and hence prohibition), a "primary sense" and a "secondary sense." Åqvist's solution also turns out to be inadequate.[18]

6. Solution to the Good Samaritan Paradox.

Given the system SDL^-, it is possible to resolve

the Good Samaritan paradox in a simple manner. In
Chapter IV, we introduce a deontic system S which
contains a primitive dyadic operator $O(/)$. Within the
system S, the paradox is automatically resolved.
There are other good reasons for using the dyadic
operator which we shall explain in Chapter IV. The
fact that the paradox is automatically resolved in the
system S will be discussed after we introduce our
solution to this paradox.

    The problem with the paradox arises when one
attempts to state sentence (2) formally.

(2)   It ought to be the case that the Samaritan helps
Jones whom Smith has robbed.

Let us study sentence (2). The obligation described
by (2) is satisfied exactly when the Samaritan helps
Jones. That Smith has robbed Jones is not a part of
this obligation. It is only a piece of additional
information, a circumstance surrounding the Samaritan's
obligation to help Jones. Hence the correct way to
state (2) formally would be:

(2") $OB \wedge A$.

The way of stating (2) emphasizes the exact extent of
the obligation. It also mentions the circumstance that
Smith robbed Jones without confusing the circumstance
with the obligation. In the traditional formalization
of the paradox, (2) was stated formally as:

(2') $O(B \wedge A)$.

This formalization indicated, contrary to the intent
of the original English sentence (2), that the
obligation being described is a complex one. It
covers both helping Jones and robbing him. Clearly
such a representation of (2) is inadequate, and
consequently, it is no surprise that it leads to
unacceptable results. The representation is motivated
by a superficial examination of sentence (2). In this
sentence the expression "it ought to be the case"
precedes the rest of the sentence, hence, it is
hastily assumed that whatever comes after the

expression is a part of the described obligation.

The problem here stems from the English language which, in this case, does not provide adequate punctuation to delineate the scope of O. Hence, the scope of O in sentence (2) is ambiguous between a wide one ranging over the whole sentence and a narrow one ranging over the first conjunct only. But further examination of the sentence reveals the correct scope. Here, when the scope of O is mistaken for the wide one, the paradox appears. When the scope of O is understood properly as limited to the first conjunct, the paradox cannot be formulated since the new formal counterpart to (2) will become:

(2") OB∧A

and clearly this does not yield OA which leads to the paradox.

In some versions of this paradox, the scope of the O-operator is defined correctly, but a false principle which appears very similar to (DR1) is used to get the paradoxical result.[19] The principle states that:

$$\frac{\vdash (A \land B) \to C}{\vdash (A \land OB) \to OC} \ .$$

That this principle is false is revealed by those versions of the Good Samaritan paradox. Indeed, those versions are not paradoxes at all but simply counter-examples to the false principle above. This principle is anyway invalid in all of the standard systems of deontic logic.

It is now clear that the language of SDL⁻ is adequate for resolving the Good Samaritan paradox without any new additions like those suggested by Rickman and Robison, for example.

Since the problem behind the Good Samaritan paradox has been revealed, there is no reason to treat it again with respect to our system S. But it is interesting to note here that the dyadic operator O(/)

eliminates the ambiguity faced in SDL⁻ altogether. So that the problem would not arise even for an unsuspecting translator. The slash in O(/) separates the circumstance of the ought-statement from the statement itself. Therefore, in this case, (2) will be expressed in this new terminology as:

O(B/A).

The problem of the ambiguity of scope is clearly avoided here.

B. A Resolution of the Second Group of Paradoxes in Deontic Logic

1. A Proposed Resolution of Plato's Paradox.

Many philosophers have found this paradox simple to resolve. Lemmon himself, who presented this specific version of the paradox, concluded that it is "evidently resolved by not returning the gun."[20] He then suggests several methods for arriving at such a conclusion. One of the more salient suggestions requires the existence of an ordering of our various duties and obligations, such that in cases of conflict all one needs to do is fulfill the obligation or duty ranking highest in the ordering. Baier makes a similar suggestion in his book <u>The Moral Point of View</u>; while Castañeda discusses in great detail a theory of morality involving a hierarchy of norms that purports to resolve conflicts. Castañeda's solution to conflicts will be singled out for discussion later since it represents the most detailed and precise proposal.[21] An observant reader will immediately point out that given our aim of defending (A1), such solutions to the paradox as the ones listed above cannot be accepted. These solutions assume as their starting point that obligations do indeed conflict, contrary to (A1). It is on the basis of this assumption that a method is consequently advanced to resolve the conflicts. We now show that such an observation stems from a confusion based on a serious ambiguity in the deontic language.

2. The Notions of "Actual" and "Prima Facie" Obligations and their Role in Plato's Paradox.

We shall use David Ross' discussions of "actual obligation" or "obligation sans phrase" and "prima facie obligation" in the <u>The Foundations of Ethics</u> and <u>The Right and the Good</u> as a starting point for our detailed study of the notions of "actual ought-statement" and "prima facie ought-statement."[22]

According to Ross, an actual obligation is an obligation which is grounded in the totality of considerations relating to the whole situation pertaining to that obligation. On the other hand, a prima facie obligation is grounded in considerations relating only to certain aspects of the situation. Ross argues that

> For while an act may well be prima facie obligatory in respect of one character and prima facie forbidden in virtue of another, it becomes obligatory or forbidden only in virtue of the totality of its ethically relevant characteristics.[23]

When all the aspects of the situation are considered, a prima facie obligation may be overridden, i.e., the total aspects of the situation may reveal that the prima facie disobligatoriness of the state of affairs described by the obligation, outweighs its prima facie obligatoriness and, thus, this prima facie obligation will not become an actual obligation once all the aspects have been considered. Hence, a prima facie obligation expresses only the tendency of a state of affairs to be obligatory.[24]

This fact about prima facie obligations led Ross to deny that they are a kind of obligation,

> [the phrase "prima facie obligation"] seems to say that prima facie obligations are one kind of obligation, while they are in fact something different; for we are not obliged to do that which is only

> prima facie obligatory. We are bound
> to do that act whose prima facie
> obligatoriness in those respects in
> which it is prima facie obligatory
> most outweighs its prima facie dis-
> obligatoriness in those respects in
> which it is prima facie disobligatory.[25]

Let us illustrate this point.

Suppose that you found a deserted infant in the park, crying of hunger. Based on this aspect of the siutation, you have a prima facie obligation to give the infant a bottle of milk. But suppose further that the infant is wearing a medical tag which informs you that he is allergic to milk but not to juice. Assuming that there are no further morally relevant aspects to this situation, you can conclude on the basis of the totality of considerations relating to the whole situation (e.g., that the infant is deserted, that you found him, that he is hungry, that you ought to feed him, that he is allergic to milk but not to juice) that you have an actual obligation to give the infant juice.

This conclusion clearly illustrates the fact that a prima facie obligation is not an obligation but one step in the process of determining what is an obligation given a certain situation.

Similarly, we shall now define an actual ought-statement as one which is based on the totality of considerations relating to the whole situation, while a prima facie ought-statement is based only on certain aspects of the situation. Baier speaks of prima facie ought-statements as presumptions which can be rebutted or confirmed after considering the whole situation. But until then they remain presumptions and consequently do not entail what ought or ought not to be the case.[26] Hence, Baier takes a line akin to ours and Ross'; he denies that prima facie ought-statements are a kind of an ought-statement.

It is easy to confuse the notions of prima facie and actual obligation with those of apparent and real obligation. To eliminate any such confusion, we emphasize what Ross said in pointing out the drawbacks of his choice of the term "prima facie":

> 'Prima' facie suggests that one is speaking only of an appearance which a moral situation presents at first sight, and which may turn out to be illusory; whereas what I am speaking of is an objective fact involved in the nature of the situation or more strictly in an element of its nature...[27]

The fact that a prima facie obligation has an objective foundation in the nature of the situation and is not a mere illusion can be shown easily in cases where the aspects of the situation under consideration are themselves complex. The complexity of an aspect leads to a thorough process of deliberation (which will be discussed in later sections) in order to determine which prima facie obligations are, in fact, based on this aspect. Consequently, it is clear that results reached in such cases are not reached at first sight; they are not illusions. They are very well considered results that have been reached on the basis of a set of considerations. In cases where that set of considerations represents the total situation, the process of deliberation mentioned above specifies, in fact, the actual obligations. This fact reveals that the problem lies not with the process of deliberation itself--it is not a first glance--but with the scope of considerations used in that process to determine the obligations. No further deliberation--nor a second glance-- will make a prima facie obligation "disappear" so long as the original scope of considerations remains constant. Consequently, a prima facie obligation is as objectively- and reality-based on its grounds, as is an actual obligation based on the total situation. A similar conclusion can be reached with respect to prima facie and actual ought-statements.

This concludes our comments on the distinction between actual and prima facie ought-statements. We are prepared now to return to Plato's paradox and reexamine it in light of these notions. Given one aspect of the situation described in the paradox, namely that we promised our friend to return his gun, we can assert the following prima facie ought-statement: we ought to return the gun to our friend. On the other hand, given another aspect of the situation, namely that our friend wants to kill his wife with the gun, we can assert another prima facie ought-statement: we ought not to return the gun to our friend. Now both these statements are well considered presumptions waiting to be rebutted or confirmed in the light of the real situation. Considerations of the total situation rebut the first prima facie ought-statement while confirming the second. This result is in accordance with Lemmon's intuitions on how this conflict must be resolved.[28]

Since ought-statements, as ordinarily stated, are ambiguous, i.e., it is not usually clear whether they are prima facie or actual ought-statements, (A1) can be interpreted in two important ways which have been responsible for the confusion on whether (A1) is valid or not. If (A1) is taken to be a statement concerning prima facie ought-statements, it is obviously false. Plato's paradox is an adequate counter-example to it. On the other hand, if (A1) is taken to be as a statement concerning actual obligation, then we claim, it is valid. Plato's paradox cannot be used in this instance as a counter-example to (A1). As a matter of fact, by suggesting his solution to the paradox, Lemmon removed the last possibility of using it against (A1). It should be clear that strictly speaking the only proper interpretation of (A1) is the latter. This is so because (A1) is proposed as an axiom of deontic logic, or the logic of obligations. Prima facie obligations are not obligations and, hence, any statement concerning them does not belong to deontic logic. What we are defending in this work can now be clearly stated as the set of proposed axioms for a logic of obligations, or more emphatically, a logic of actual obligations. It is not our intention to argue that prima facie ought-statements do not conflict. That they do is obvious. But that is no ground for rejecting (A1). If (A1) is to be rejected, a case of conflicting actual ought-statements must be produced.

In the next section we show how the ambiguity in ought-statements has caused the rejection of another major principle.

3. An Examination of Some Arguments against the Principle that "Ought" Implies "Can".

  a. Lemmon's Arguments. For philosophers who misinterpret (A1) as pertaining to prima facie ought-statements, and consequently reject it, the possibility of rejecting the Kantian principle "ought" implies "can" is greatly increased. This is due to the fact that since they accept that prima facie ought-statements conflict, then they can assert on the basis of (A2) that $(OA \land O\sim A) \rightarrow O(A \land \sim A)$. This result obviously goes against the Kantian principle.

  Such a line of reasoning for rejecting this principle was, in fact, given by Lemmon, who then concluded that the Kantian principle and (A1) "stand or fall together."[29] In another article he offers yet another argument against the principle that "ought" implies "can":

> If X ought to do A, and ought to do B, then X ought to do A and B, by a principle of deontic logic which I and others accept; hence in the cases under consideration, X ought to do both A and not-A; now if 'ought' implies 'can', it follows that X can do both A and not-A, and yet it is a logical truth that X cannot do both A and not-A.[30]

  Thus the crux of Lemmon's case against the Kantian principle is the claim that ought-statements do conflict. In examining his examples of cases where ought-statements are claimed to conflict, including his version of Plato's paradox, it seems that they all run afoul of the distinction introduced in the earlier section. Here is one such example:

> I ought to burn these manuscripts (the poet made me promise to do so on his

> deathbed), but I simply cannot (of
> course I have the physical and
> psychological power--it is just that
> my aesthetic sense would be outraged
> by the act).[31]

This example, like Plato's paradox, clearly formulates prima facie ought-statements. That these are prima facie ought-statements is obvious from the parenthetical remarks that Lemmon feels necessary to introduce in order to make sense of this conflict. These remarks make it clear that each ought-statement is based on an analysis of only one aspect of the situation and hence can only be a presumption or a prima facie ought-statement. It is not unusual, therefore, that conflict ensues. Lemmon has failed to show us a conflict of actual ought-statements. He only showed us a conflict of prima facie ought-statements. This possibility of prima facie ought-statements conflicting with each other was never contested. But Lemmon disagrees with this conclusion.

> It may be argued that these are merely
> prima facie obligations, one of which
> will 'disappear' when our true moral
> situation, what we 'really' ought to
> do, has been revealed to us. This
> view seems to me to make the moral
> life too easy. Perhaps Ross' term
> prima facie is here ill-judged; rather
> it is essential to our perplexity
> when faced with conflicting obliga-
> tions that we really are under an
> obligation to do A and also under one
> to do not-A (e.g., we really did give
> conflicting promises).[32]

Clearly, Lemmon's argument against our conclusion is rooted in another confusion we warned against in the previous section. Here, Lemmon confuses "prima facie" with "apparent" or "that which may turn out to be illusory." Hence, his reference to "disappearing" obligations. He illustrates his claim that the conflict of obligations is real by pointing out that "e.g., we really did give conflicting promises." But this correct observation shows only that prima facie obligations conflict. It does not show them unreal. The reality and absoluteness of an obligation must not be confused. "Prima facie" as we argued earlier, refers to "an objective fact involved in the nature of the situation." Nevertheless, a prima facie obligation may be rebutted in a specific situation. Therefore, Lemmon's rejection of the view that conflicting obligations are only prima facie obligations, is based on his misunderstanding of the concept of "prima facie." Given our analyses, Lemmon has failed to present a case of conflicting actual ought-statements. Consequently, his arguments against (A1) and the Kantian principle are ineffective.

b. Hare's Arguments. Hare furnishes many cases "in which 'ought' can be as it were, weakened so as no longer to possess the property which makes 'ought' and 'cannot' disagree."[33] One such case is where "I ought to go and see him" is taken to mean "there is a moral convention that people in my situation should go and see him." Another is where "I ought to go and see him" means "as a matter of psychological fact I shall feel guilty if I do not go and see him." Hare claims that:

> So used, 'ought' by no means implies 'can'; for in many cases people are unable to do what moral convention requires, and in many cases they feel guilt, or remorse, for their failure to do actions which they know to have been impossible.[34]

Each of the above ought-statements, given by Hare as cases where "ought" does not imply "can," is based on some aspect of the situation under consideration, and not on the whole situation. Hare himself supplies that aspect in presenting each case. Therefore, clearly, these are cases of prima facie ought-statements.

The principle "ought" implies "can," like (A1), is ambiguous between two main interpretations corresponding to the two notions: "actual ought" and "prima

52

facie ought." That prima facie "oughts" do not always imply "can" is a clear consequence of Plato's paradox if these prima facie "oughts" obey a principle analogous to that expressed by (A2). Therefore, Hare's cases do not refute the Kantian principle when interpreted as pertaining to actual "oughts." Furthermore, it is useless to consider such cases as a way of discovering the validity of the principle under the interpretation referred to in the previous sentence, and which is the sole interpretation which falls within the scope of deontic logic. For, suppose that we try to discover the actual "ought" in these cases. To do that we have to consider the totality of each situation. Suppose that this totality includes in the first case the following aspect of the situation: that we are unable in this case to do what moral convention requires (because a court decision has put me under house arrest). Suppose that there are no additional relevant aspects here. If one accepts the Kantian principle, considerations of the situation as a whole will lead to deny the following ought-statement: we ought to go and see him. Therefore, the result of this case does not contradict the Kantian principle. On the other hand, if one rejects the Kantian principle, then he will assert the following actual ought-statement: we ought to go and see him. Consequently, such cases offer no help in rebutting or affirming the principle. Nor do the feelings of guilt and remorse offer us any clue as to the validity of the principle that "ought" implies "can"; since not only is it the case that people can misjudge their obligations, but furthermore they do sometimes indulge unjustifiably in feelings of guilt. The latter aspect represents a psychological problem not relevant to the principles of deontic logic. We conclude this discussion by emphasizing that neither Lemmon nor Hare has supplied counter-examples to the principle that "ought" implies "can." A belief to the contrary rests on a confusion between prima facie and actual "ought." Our principle, as a deontic principle pertains to actual "oughts" only, and any counter-example to its analogue pertaining to prima facie "oughts" is irrelevant.

4. An Exploration of Castañeda's Method for Solving Plato's Paradox.

In an earlier section we said that Lemmon and others suggested the use of a preexisting ordering of our obligations, or the principles on which they rest, as a way for resolving conflicts of duties. We also said that since Castañeda offers the most detailed proposal for constructing such a hierarchy, we shall single out his proposal for discussion. This is our present task.

The proposal was expounded in "A Theory of Morality." In this article Castañeda describes his ethical system as "very comprehensive; it contains every other normative system as a proper subsystem."[35] The nonethical systems encompass all kinds of norms, e.g., courtesy rules, football rules, laws, etc. These systems are arranged in an ethical hierarchy. To distinguish the ethical "ought" from the non-ethical "ought" he uses numerical subscripts for the latter only. The ethical ought enjoins the doing of action prescribed by norms belonging to a subsystem in the hierarchy. In cases of conflict of duties, the ethical "ought" enjoins the doing of the action prescribed by the higher subsystem. Formally, the unsubscripted, ethical "ought" is defined as follows:

(E) A ought to be done if and only if there is an i such that ought$_i$ to be done, and there is no j smaller than i such that A is forbidden$_j$.

The subscript i denotes the place of the normative subsystem in the ethical hierarchy. Higher subsystems have subscripts with smaller values.[36]

The contents of morality, according to Castañeda are to be found in the principles governing the ranking of these subsystems. Let us explain the process by which this ranking is achieved in Castañeda's system. "The moral value of a norm N is the moral value of the class of actions prescribed by N."[37] The moral value of the class of actions prescribed by N is, in turn, dependent on the moral value of its members. We have now reached the most elementary and fundamental step in building the ethical hierarchy--the moral value of an action, which is defined by Castañeda as a function of an "emotional quality" possessed by the action and referred to as "satisfaction."[38]

At this point it seems that conflicts of duties, which involve actions having different moral values, can be solved in a straightforward manner by computing the moral values of each action, and performing that which has the highest moral value. But although Castañeda assumes that such values can be computed, he chooses another method for solving conflicts of duties. According to this method the moral value of individual actions is used to determine the moral value of classes of actions which, in turn, is used to determine the moral value of the different norms and to arrange them in a hierarchy, within the subsystems. The subsystems themselves are then ranked in the final hierarchy on the basis of the moral value of the class of norms belonging to each of them.[39]

Once the hierarchy is established it becomes for Castañeda the sole criterion for making moral decisions, as is revealed by definition (E) above. It is then subject to change only for three reasons: a) if it turns out that the hierarchy contains inconsistent norms, b) if there is a gap to be filled in the ordering, or c) if the hierarchy is proven to be inconsistent in that a subsystem S whose moral value is higher than that of S' is ranked below S'.[40]

Given Castañeda's hierarchy, the solution of Plato's paradox in his system will not depend on the moral value of the action of giving a gun as compared to that of not giving it, but on the moral value of the subsystem to which the norms prescribing these actions belong. In this case, "you ought to return the gun" prescribing the return of the gun, can be regarded as a norm belonging to the subsystem of social conventions. "You ought not to return the gun" prescribing not returning the gun, can be regarded as a norm belonging to the legal subsystem. If we accept the assumption that the moral value of the legal subsystem ranks higher than that of social convention, (a reasonable assumption), we can conclude that the ethical "ought" enjoins the act of not returning the gun. This resolution of the conflict is consistent with our moral intuitions. Castañeda's system succeeds in resolving Plato's paradox.

5. Criticism of Castañeda's Method.

But though Castañeda's method resolved successfully Plato's paradox, it is a complete failure in resolving other types of conflict of duties. Furthermore in some cases where the resolution of the conflict lies clearly in following a certain course of action, Castañeda's method yield results to the contrary.

Let us consider the first charge. In constructing Castañeda's system, it is assumed that conflict of duties originates from the fact that two different norms prescribe two incompatible actions. Hence, it is assumed that a conflict can be resolved by mere reference to the ranking of the subsystem containing each of them. But, in fact, a conflict can arise with only one norm involved. Here is an example, Joe is watching his twin sons drown. He cannot save both of them. He can only save one. The norm prescribing the action to save the first son is the same as that prescribing the action to save the second son. Since Joe cannot save both, conflict of duties arises. This conflict cannot be resolved by the usual method since there is only one norm involved. Furthermore, by (E), we can assert that "Joe ought to save the first son" as well as its conflicting counterpart, because in each case there is an i such that A ought_i to be done, and there is no j smaller than i such that A is forbidden_j. Hence, we have here a case of conflicting ethical "oughts," contrary to Castañeda's claim that only non-ethical "oughts" conflict. Similar problems can arise where two norms in the same subsystem have the same moral value, or when two subsystems have the same moral value.

We shall now substantiate the second charge against Castañeda's system, namely, that it yields in some cases results that run clearly against our moral intutitions. Consider the case of André, who is a good citizen. He votes in every election. In this instance, he ought to vote in today's mayoral elections whose result is already clear since the candidate has a landslide majority. Furthermore, in this instance, André's mother, who is very attached to her son, is on her deathbed, so André ought to stay home by his mother's side. Now suppose that political norms rank higher than familial norms, and that there are no further relevant facts about this situation.

Clearly, André is in a situation of conflict of duties, since voting requires leaving his mother's side. But the specific circumstances of this case are so clearly in favor of André staying by his mother, that most moral agents do not have to think twice about it. For, even though his political duties rank higher than familial duties, nevertheless, the moral value of voting in this instance is negligibly low, while the moral value of staying by his mother's side is tremendously high. Our moral sense would then resolve this conflict by stating that Andre ought to stay by his mother's side.

But Castañeda's method yields the opposite answer. What matters in this method is not the moral value of the action but that of the subsystem. In this case, the political subsystem ranks higher than the subsystem of familial norms, consequently, by (E), André ought to vote.

The reason behind this unacceptable result, lies in the fact that a class of actions can have an enormously high moral value even when one of its members has a dismally low moral value. This is so because the moral value of the class of actions, according to Castañeda, is simply the sum of the moral values of individual actions. So that, if there are some actions of unusually high moral value, they will compensate for the one with the low moral value. Since norms and consequently, subsystems depend in their ranking on the moral value of the class of actions belonging to each norm; everything else being equal, this action with the unusual low moral value will be prescribed by a norm belonging to a subsystem of a higher moral value. On the other hand, everything else being equal, an action with exactly the opposite characteristic, i.e., it has a high moral value in a class of actions which have low moral values, will be prescribed by a norm belonging to a subsystem of a lower moral value. So in case of conflict of duties involving the two actions described, the higher norm will prescribe the action having the lower moral value. A similar problem arises where the discrepancy between the moral value of a norm and that of the class to which it belongs is also great. In either of these cases the system yields results that clash with our moral intuitions.

Castañeda's system is not concerned with the particulars; the particular situation, particular action, or particular norm. Its basic concern is the average case. Therefore, sharp variations from the average case yield the unintuitive results discussed above. This excessive abstraction from the specificity of the moral situation leads Castañeda's system to even less palatable results. Take a set of subsystems. Call them S_1, S_2, S_3. Let $S1 = \{N_3, N_5, N_8\}$, $S_2 = \{N_1, N_4, N_8\}$ and $S_3 = \{N_1, N_3, N_7\}$. Let the moral value of $N_1 = 1$, $N_2 = 2$ and so on.

Since the subsystems are ranked in the hierarchy on the basis of the moral value of the class of norms belonging to each of them it is clear that in this example S_1 ranks higher than S_2 which ranks higher than S_3. As Castañeda's convention demands, we have assigned to the higher subsystems subscripts with smaller values.

Suppose now that S_1 is the subsystem of military laws, S_2 is the subsystem of social conventions, while S_3 is that of courtesy; and suppose that you are in a situation of conflict between an action prescribed by a courtesy rule N_3 and a norm of social convention N_8. Now N_8 belongs to S_2 which is higher than S_3 to which N_3 belongs. But on the other hand, N_3 belongs to S_1 which has nothing to do with the situation but satisfies the description of being the highest subsystem. Hence, according to Castañada the ethical "ought" enjoins the action prescribed by N_3 which belongs to the highest subsystem.

Our various examples above have shown the serious inadequacies of Castañeda's method for resolving conflicts. It is important to note that at least the first part of our criticism pertaining to conflicts based on the same norm, or norms belonging to sub-systems of equal moral value can be generalized so as to apply to hierarchies other than that of Castañeda.

6. The Special Significance of Sartre's Paradox.

In light of our discussion of the possiblity of solving conflicts of duties by reference to a pre-existing ethical hierarchy, Sartre's paradox acquires added significance. It represents one further illustration of the fact that the specificity of a moral case cannot be always ignored in determining one's duties. For, although we may admit that political norms generally rank higher than familial norms, we still have to determine in complex moral situations whether the specific case under consideration is one which obeys this general ranking of norms or is the exception to it. As Mill pointed out:

> It is not the fault of any creed, but of the complicated nature of human affairs, that rules of conduct cannot be so framed as to require no exceptions, and that hardly any kind of action can safely be laid down as either always obligatory, or always condemnable.[41]

Consequently, even if a norm N_1 generally ranks higher than another norm N_2, the exception to norm N_1 may rank quite differently with respect to instances or exceptions of norm N_2. This is the aspect which complicates the resolution of moral dilemmas; and this aspect is not recognized in solutions, based on preexisting hierarchies, of the sort discussed earlier. Hare agrees,

> Sartre uses the example in order to make the point that in such cases no antecedently 'existing' principle can be appealed to... . We have to consider the particular case and make

> up our minds what are its morally
> relevant features, and what, taking
> these features into account, ought to
> be done in such a case. Nevertheless,
> when we do make up our minds, it is
> about a matter of principle which has
> a bearing outside the particular case.[42]

We would like to make two remarks pertaining to Hare's, as well as to the earlier discussion. While rejecting the use of preexisting ethical hierarchies for providing an automatic solution of moral dilemmas, which consists solely of checking the comparative ranking of the norms involved and deciding accordingly, we do not reject preexisting ethical hierarchies. Human beings usually do uphold that certain moral principles are higher than others. They do uphold some sort of an ethical hierarchy which can be crude or sophisticated depending on the individual. Hence, when faced with a moral dilemma, they do have some information to fall back on. But in the case of the sophisticated moral agent, this ethical hierarchy is regarded by him as a generally working hierarchy which resolves most but not all conflicts. Therefore, he would be judicious in his use of this hierarchy, and alert for any exceptional moral conflicts that may come along. In the latter case new methods and new information have to be introduced as we shall see later.

Secondly, we agree with Hare that even when we resolve an exceptional case of moral dilemma, our resolution has a bearing outside the particular case. This is so because our resolution might reveal that our hierarchies need refinement. Furthermore, when the resolution of several moral dilemmas concerning the same norms turns out to be consistently contrary to that based exclusively on the ranking of the norms within the hierarchy, then an alert moral agent might reconsider and, consequently, restructure his hierarchy, in light of the accumulated evidence. Hence, not only does the hierarchy affect the resolution of the specific case, but also, an accumulation of information based on the resolution of the specific case can affect the hierarchy.

Another reason to bestow added significance upon Sartre's paradox is due to the fact that if we fail to resolve convincingly the conflict in this paradox, then our earlier distinction between prima facie and actual obligation will not be adequate to stave off this attack on (A1), since we could end up here with two conflicting actual ought-statements. Consequently, we would have to reject (A1). As inadequate as it was, the solution by referring solely to a hierarchy, did resolve Plato's paradox. Yet, having shown the inadequacy of the solution, we are now standing with a new and more powerful paradox in our hands, but with no solution. To decree at this point that Sartre's paradox involves only prima facie and not actual ought-statements is a lame defense unless, a) we can point out the actual obligations, b) argue conclusively that, indeed, these are the actual obligations, and that furthermore, c) they do not conflict. Such tasks are not as easy to perform in this case as they were in the case of Plato's paradox.

7. Some General Observations Concerning Prima Facie and Actual Ought-Statements.

a. The Moral Weight of an Ought-Statement. When a norm N_1 ranks higher than a norm N_2, we shall say that N_1 carries greater moral weight than N_2. When two norms are involved in a case of conflict of duties, the comparative weights of these norms helps settle the conflict but need not be the sole factor in settling it as we saw earlier. This is due to the fact that each instance of a norm derives its own moral weight at least partially, from that norm. Consequently, the moral weights of the instances involved in a conflict of duties can themselves be compared, thus making the resolution of the conflict more accessible.

Similarly, the specific circumstances in a situation under consideration also affect the moral weight of an instance (of some norm) involved in that situation. This is what we meant when we argued along with Hare that no preexisting ethical hierarchy is alone adequate for resolving complex moral conflict. The details of the situation could reveal that the higher norm involved in the situation is involved in it only tangentially. They could also reveal, as we argued earlier that this specific instance of the norm has an exceptionally high, or low moral value, as the case may be. Consider André's situation.[43] It is generally true that it ought to be the case that André votes. But compare the following two circumstances: a) where the vote concerns a mayoral election whose result is for all purposes settled, with not much hanging on this result; and b) where the vote concerns a tight race for the presidency of the country, and where the result could alter the country's political structure. In the absence of other factors, it is clear that in both cases: it ought to be the case that André votes. But circumstance b) lends a higher weight to this ought-statement than circumstance a). To see this, suppose André is in a situation where he has to choose between voting in the mayoral election and voting in the presidential election. The right decision is immediately obvious. It ought to be the case that André votes in the presidential election. The urgency of the presidential election lends added weight to the ought-statement, while the blandness of the mayoral election does not add any weight to the ought-statement; perhaps it detracts from it instead. Consequently, we should be able to talk about the comparative weights of ought-statements, and to use this information for resolving conflicts between prima facie ought-statements.

b. The Role of Circumstances in Determining Obligations. The second observation that we would like to make concerns the role of the circumstances in a situation in determining what actually ought to be the case. This observation is closely related to the first, because by modifying the moral weight of a prima facie ought-statement, the circumstances can create a discrepancy between the moral weights of conflicting prima facie ought-statements that could result in determining what is the actual ought-statement. Consider Sartre's example again. The paradox there derives its force from the assumption that Sartre has related to us all the morally relevant circumstances of the situation and left nothing out. For suppose that situation was as described by Sartre except for the additional fact that the son had also five other siblings to whom the mother is also greatly attached and who are willing to stay by her side. Clearly, such a factor reduces the force of the dilemma greatly. It introduces another aspect to the situation by introducing a new circumstance, which decreases the moral weight of one of the conflicting statements, the statement that it ought to be the case that you stay by your mother's side.

Now suppose that we investigate the situation further and discover that all the five siblings of this person have just been jailed by the occupying forces. This new fact reverses the previous situation and brings back the earlier conflict of duty in fuller force, since now the mother is pictured as one burdened with the pain of having been separated in her last days from all her children but one. On the other hand, the fight for one's country carries a more concrete and urgent meaning for the son since he now associates it also with the resolution of his new familial tragedy. Under the new description of the situation we witness an escalation of the conflict. The conflict is still in effect but the moral weight of each ought-statement is increased.

We can go on further and imagine additional facts about the situation that could anull the conflict even at this escalated level and so on. The important fact to remember is that all we did with Sartre's example was to add to bits of morally relevant information, without disposing of old ones. By adding information we changed the moral description of the situation. Similar results can be obtained by removing circumstances in a situation, instead of adding them. This shows the crucial role of specifying the circumstances of a moral situation. The truth of each prima facie ought-statement is conditional upon those aspects of the situation on which it is based. Similarly, the truth of an actual ought-statement is conditional upon the totality of aspects of the situation in which it was asserted. This fact led W. J. Rees to argue:

> Our moral rules...appear to conflict
> ...only because we mistakenly try to

analyze them in terms of unconditional rather than conditional statements. When they are regarded as concealed conditional statements, an adequate analysis of the conditions will always remove the possibility of conflict.[44]

Our resolution of Sartre's paradox in this chapter, will indeed be based on an adequate analysis of the conditions.

At this point, we have to point out an apparent tension in Ross' discussion of prima facie and actual obligation. He refers at one time to prima facie obligation as conditional, while he refers later to actual obligation as absolute.[45] This reference seems inconsistent with Ross' own definition of both notions. It is true that a prima facie obligation is conditional upon a specific aspect of the situation. But it is also true that an actual obligation is conditional upon all aspects of the situation as Ross himself acknowledges.[46] Hence, the same considerations that lead us to recognize prima facie obligation as conditional also lead us to recognize actual obligation as conditional.

But in Ross' work, the characteristic of being an absolute obligation is not opposed to that of being a conditional one. At one place he says that an obligation is absolute if it admits of no exceptions.[47] In this sense, prima facie obligations are not absolute. The fact that they only tend to be true illustrates this fact. By the same token, actual obligations are indeed absolute. They do not only tend to be true, but furthermore they are true every time. They admit of no exceptions, because they cannot be overriden. In this sense, actual obligations are absolute; but this is consistent with the assertion that they are conditional in form. "Absolute" in Ross' terminology, does not mean "unconditional"; it only means "admitting of no exception."

8. The Complexity of Determining an Actual Ought-Statement on the Basis of Prima Facie Ones.

a. Considerations of the Situation as a Whole May Rebut all the Prima Facie Ought-Statements Related to that Situation. Given a circumstance C_1, suppose that we can assert on its basis the following prima facie ought-statement: It ought to be the case that A. Similarly, given a circumstance C_2, suppose that we can assert on its basis the following prima facie ought-statement: It ought to be the case that B. Now given $(C_1 \wedge C_2)$, it should be clear from our discussion in the previous section, that we cannot conclude automatically from the above either that it ought to be the case that A or that it ought to be the case that B.

We contend further, that as a totality $(C_1 \wedge C_2)$ can lead to deontic assertions that are quite different from either of the presumptions asserted on the basis of C_1 alone or C_2 alone.

Consider an example introduced earlier about a man called Joe who is wathcing his two sons drowning. Let us modify the example in the following way: If Joe jumps into the water to save his children, he can save only one child, and the process would take him two and a half minutes. Joe is standing near an emergency phone. It takes a minute to make the phone call, and two minutes for help to arrive and save both sons. Suppose now that the two sons can survive until summoned help arrives but only at the cost of being hospitalized.

The first aspect of the situation relates to the first son. He is drowning and his father can save him within two and a half minutes without the son needing to be hospitalized. Since no one should be made to suffer needlessly, we reach the following prima facie ought-statements: It ought to be the case that Joe jumps into the water and saves his first son. Call this OA. The second aspect is identical to the first in all respects but one; it relates to the second son. Here we reach by the same token, a similar conclusion about saving the second son, call it OB. Putting the situation together as a whole, by putting together the two aspects C_1 and C_2 will reveal that we have here a prima facie conflict of duty, since saving either child by jumping into the water will prevent saving the other, by our assumption. So, it seems that we need to analyze the situation further in order to determine which of these two prima facie ought-statements will be rebutted, and which will be confirmed.

But reviewing the situation as an organic whole reveals that both prima facie ought-statements are rebutted in this case. When considering each aspect of the situation separately, we could not justify leaving that son, under consideration, in the water until help arrives. That would have caused him unnecessary suffering. But in light of the situation as a whole (in light of the fact that both sons are drowning, that each presumption, if confirmed, would save only one son, that both sons can be saved at the price of additional but bearable suffering) new norms and ethical principles become involved in the new situation. These norms and principles were not previously involved in any of the separate aspects of that situation, e.g., that it is better to save both sons than just one, that justified suffering is permissible. The totality of all these considerations, old as well as new, make it clear that the actual ought-statement based on all of them is neither OA nor OB. It is OD, where D is the state of affairs where Joe calls for help. Obviously, OD is quite different from either OA or OB. This establishes our claim.

The fact that a complex situation can lead to deontic assertions that differ significantly from the presumptions based on the separate aspects of that situation must be used with great care. It should not lead us to regard as useless a very beneficial method employed often in the theory and practice of morality, namely, the method of breaking up a morally complex situation into smaller more manageable parts. But it should caution us as to the limitations of this method. We shall now explore these limitations.

Given a complex situation, consider the prima facie ought-statement based on one of its aspects. If the remaining circumstances, not included in that aspect, are all irrelevant to this prima facie ought-statement, then this prima facie ought-statement is an actual ought-statement in that situation. We shall say that a circumstance C_1 is irrelevant to the prima facie ought statement OA whenever OA is not rebutted, nor is its weight changed by the addition of C_1 to the aspect of the situation on which OA is based.

On the other hand, if a circumstance C_1 is relevant to a prima facie ought-statement OA in a certain situation, then C_1 has to be considered in order to determine whether OA is to be rebutted or confirmed. In this case, the breakup method can yield prima facie ought-statements that are quite different from the actual ought-statements of that situation.

Often the answer to the question of whether a specific circumstance in a situation is relevant to a prima facie ought-statement based on an aspect not involving this circumstance, is immediately obvious. But where the answer is not obvious, the moral agent has to go through the actual process of considering the effects of the circumstance being considered on the prima facie ought-statements based on those aspects that do not include this circumstance. Therefore, in cases where each circumstance in the situation is obviously irrelevant to the prima facie ought-statements based on the aspects not including that circumstance, the method of breaking up the deontic situation can be counted on to yield directly the actual ought-statements in that situation. It will not fail. But, in all other cases, it can be used only as a preliminary step for clarifying the various aspects of a deontic situation. Consequently, in these cases, its preliminary results must be checked further.

     b. Considerations of the Situation as a Whole May Lead a Moral Agent to Change the Situation. As just argued, adding a new circumstance to the aspect of the situation on which a prima facie ought-statement rests, can drastically change the resulting ought-statement. With some ingenuity, a moral agent can use this fact favorably.

     Consider a situation S. Suppose that the actual ought-statement, which is based on all aspects of S, as an integrated whole, is OA. By producing a new circumstance, C, the new situation becomes (S∧C), so that S no more represents the total situation. Consequently, OA cannot be asserted in (S∧C) as an actual ought-statement without being reassessed in light of all the new aspects. As we saw earlier, by choosing the suitable C, OA can now be rebutted, and the agent can escape the obligation expressed by OA.

There is a story in the literature of deontic logic which can illustrate this option; at the same time it draws our attention to the necessity of defining clearly the acceptable limits of such escapism. The story is that of Suzy Mae, who was impregnated by John Doe.[48] Upon finding out that Suzy was pregnant, John shot her. In the original story it is not clear why John reacted in this manner;but it is stated there that upon shooting Suzy, it was no longer true that: It ought to be the case that John marries Suzy. Hence, we can amplify the original version by assuming that John killed Suzy in order to eliminate the obligation expressed by that ought-statement. He clearly succeeded. But obviously, what John did is not acceptable from a moral point of view. Therefore, we must define the limits of such an alternative.

If the new circumstance, to be added to the original situation is one which the moral agent can produce, and if producing it creates a new situation which is not as good as the situation that would have resulted had the moral agent fulfilled his obligations, then it is clear that it ought not to be the case that such a circumstance is produced. On the other hand, if producing it creates a new situation which is morally better than the one that could have resulted had the agent fulfilled his old obligations, then it ought to be the case that the circumstance is produced.

Having drawn the reader's attention in this section, to some of the complexities involved in determining one's actual obligations, we are now prepared to discuss our solution to Sartre's paradox.

9. Solution to the Second Group of Paradoxes.

a. Plato's Paradox. In Section 6, we argued that an ethical hierarchy is useful in resolving many conflicts, but that it must be used with care. Resolution of conflicts may not be made automatically on the basis of this hierarchy alone. The particular details of the situation must be taken into consideration. The case of Plato's paradox is one where the solution can be straightforwardly based on the hierarchy. The principle of saving a person's life generally ranks higher than that of keeping a promise. The paradox provides no extenuating circumstances for modifying this ranking. Hence, the moral agent must satisfy the obligation based on the higher principle; it ought to be the case that he does not return the gun to his friend.

b. Sartre's Paradox. The solution to this paradox is less obvious than that of Plato's paradox, since the moral situation in this case is more complex. Therefore, it is advisable to analyze this paradox in a thorough and systematic manner. First we collect all the circumstances of the situation. The most salient among them are the following: Sartre's pupil has lost a brother in the war against Germany and wants to avenge him by joining the Free French Forces. His mother being deeply wounded by the death of her other son, has become greatly attached to the surviving son.

Next, we consider the various aspects of the situation. The situation can be broken up into two major aspects. The first concerns the death of the pupil's brother, and the pupil's desire to avenge him by joining the Free French Forces. This aspect produces the following prima facie ought-statements: It ought to be the case that this person joins the Free French Forces.

The second aspect concerns the mother's great attachment to this son as a result of her suffering from the death of her other son. This aspect produces, upon analysis, another prima facie ought-statement which conflicts with the first: It ought to be the case that the pupil stays with his mother.

We have now determined the prima facie ought-statements in this situation. Their weights according to Sartre are roughly equal, although their exact value cannot be determined.[49] This means that when both prima facie ought-statements are compared, neither one will outweigh the other. This is the essential difference between Sartre's paradox and Plato's paradox.

So now we consider the situation as a whole. Considerations of the situation as a whole do not produce a change in the weights of the prima facie ought-statements but it does reveal them as conflicting. At this point, someone can hastily conclude that, therefore, both prima facie ought-statements are actual ought-statements and since they conflict, we have at last produced a counter-example to (A1).

But such a conclusion is indeed hasty. The crucial part of the deliberation has only started. Granted that considerations of the situation as a whole did not rebut one prima facie ought-statement and confirm the other, still, as we argued earlier we have many more alternatives to consider. We can consider an actual ought-statement which is quite different from the above two presumptions. For example, "it ought to be the case that Sartre's pupil joins the underground in the vicinity in which his mother lives." Such a statement takes into consideration all the aspects of the situation and yet is different from the conflicting presumptions. Another solution can be conceivably based on changing this situation. But in order to preserve the thrust of Sartre's paradox, let us suppose that neither of the last two suggestions is acceptable.

Reduced to a bare minimum, this is the problem of determining an actual ought-statement solely on the basis of two conflicting prima facie ought-statements of equal weights.

A moral agent who upholds (A1) will not consider this problem as a counter-example to (A1). On the contrary, he will find the solution to it quite straightforward. When the situation is considered as a whole, it becomes clear that there is no acceptable moral criterion for choosing to confirm one presumption instead of the other. Furthermore, they cannot both be confirmed, by our initial assumption. Consequently, the actual ought-statement which takes account of all these aspects of the situation is the following: It ought to be the case that either the pupil joins the Free French Forces or stays by his mother's side. This actual ought-statement is different from either presumption, and is superior to both of them in that it takes account of the situation as a whole. The agent, according to this actual ought-statement, is free to fulfill his obligations in one of two ways. Either one is acceptable. If he still cannot decide in what way he is going to fulfill his obligations, his dilemma at this point is not a moral one.

On the other hand, a moral agent who rejects (A1) will reach a different conclusion. He will agree that when the situation is considered as a whole, there is no acceptable moral criterion for choosing to confirm one presumption instead of the other. But since he regards (A1) as false, his global considerations will lead him to confirm both. Consequently, he ends up with conflicting actual ought-statements.

In both cases discussed above--the case of the moral agent who accepts (A1) and that of the moral agent who rejects (A1)--the crucial stage of the deliberation is reached when the situation under consideration is reviewed as an organic whole. When all of the circumstances and presumptions of that situation are ultimately put together and looked upon as integreated parts of a totality, they can reveal the involvement of new norms and ethical principles, that were not originally involved when the various aspects of the situation were considered separately. When such new norms and principles are involved the resulting actual ought-statement can be different from any of the presumptions. This fact was discussed and illustrated in Section 8 above.

In Sartre's paradox, when the various circumstances and presumptions are looked upon as integrated parts of a totality, the involvement of (A1) or its negation becomes immediately clear. The two presumptions looked upon together in the context of the total situation, reveal the fact that they conflict. Consequently, considerations of the situation as a whole must take this fact into account before formulating the actual ought-statement. But this fact makes (A1), or its negation--depending on the position of the moral agent on this issue--immediately involved in those global considerations. If (A1) is accepted, then the actual ought-statement formulated reflects this fact as we saw above. If (A1) is rejected, the actual ought-statement formulated also reflects this fact. Hence, Sartre's paradox cannot be used to establish or refute (A1) without begging the question. Therefore, this paradox does not refute (A1). We have already shown above, how a moral agent who upholds (A1) resolves Sartre's paradox.

10. Other Proposed Solutions for the Second Group of Paradoxes.

    a. van Fraassen's Solution. In Section 7, we quoted Rees as saying that many of our moral rules appear to conflict because we mistakenly analyze them as unconditional rather than conditional statements. Van Fraassen is in basic agreement with Rees. The conditions of an ought-statement are made explicit in his system by the use of $O(/)$ so that $O(A/C)$ is read as: Given condition C it ought to be the case that A.[50]

Since van Fraassen refers to his logic as the logic of conditional obligation, and since a conditional version of (A1) is included as an axiom of his system, i.e.,

AC2 $\vdash$ $O(A/C) \rightarrow \sim O(\sim A/C)$ [51]

we expect his logic to deal only with actual ought-statements and not prima facie ones.

But while formulating a logic of actual obligation, van Fraassen considers in his discussion of the logic, cases of prima facie ought-statements. Such considerations which fall outside the scope of his logic, together with his wish to avoid Sartre's paradox, lead van Fraassen to modify his logic in a fundamental way. We explain this in detail in the next few sections.

In his study of the principle of detachment in deontic logic, van Fraassen considers the John and Suzy paradox.[52] This paradox is based on the following premises:

(1) John impregnated Suzy.
(2) It ought to be the case that John marries Suzy given that he impregnated her.
(3) John shot Suzy (and killed her).

From the first two premises we conclude that,

(4) It ought to be the case that John marries Suzy.

From the last premise and the deontic princple that "ought" implies "can", we conclude that,

(5) It is false that it ought to be the case that John marries Suzy.

(5) contradicts (4).

On the basis of this paradox van Fraassen argues as follows,

> Suppose that one considers what is to be done, with an eye on the moral values of the possible outcome of one's actions. Then if one knows that the actual outcome must satisfy C, and that $O(B/C)$ is true, ought one to follow a course of action leading to an outcome that satisfies B? The answer is 'no, not necessarily'; for example, one may know as well that courses of action satisfying B are not possible. This is clearly the lesson of the John and Suzy paradox.[53]

Let us examine this argument, which van Fraassen uses for the rejection of the principle of detachment, in light of our discussion in Sections B:7-8. We consider first the situation where John has impregnated Suzy but has not shot her yet. Thus the fact that John impregnated Suzy can be regarded along with our moral code as representing the totality of considerations in that situation. Consequently, one can rightly conclude in that situation that John has an actual obligation to marry Suzy, i.e., John must follow a course of action leading to his marriage to Suzy.

But instead of fulfilling his obligation John violates it by shooting and killing Suzy. The new circumstance creates a new situation with additional considerations, for example that it is (legally) impossible to marry a dead person. In light of the totality of considerations in this new situation, it is obvious that John's old obligation to marry Suzy is no longer actual. It has become in this new situation a prima facie obligation, i.e., one based on partial, not total, considerations of the new situation. Hence, it is false to assert in the new situation that John has the actual obligation to marry Suzy. John's obligation to marry Suzy ceases.

The problem with van Fraassen's analysis is that it does not bring out the fact that the paradox can be regarded as involving two consecutive but different situations. Hence his treatment of the paradox leads him to assert that John need not follow a course of action leading to his marriage with Suzy. Later the confusion is compounded when van Fraassen settles for the position that if John ought to marry Suzy given that he impregnated her, then either he ought to follow a course of action leading to his marriage with her, or at least he ought to try.[54] But surely we do not want to assert either in the case of her death.

The problem can be resolved easily by noting that the paradox can be correctly regarded in one of two ways. a) either it presents two separate situations such that the obligation to marry Suzy holds in one and not the other, hence the paradox is dissolved, or b) it presents only one situation, i.e, the final and the more complex one. In this latter case, the obligation to marry Suzy is a prima facie obligation,

hence it does not contradict the statement that it is
false that John has an actual obligation to marry Suzy.

We argued in Section B.2 that a prima facie obligation is not an obligation at all. Consequently, in formalizing deontic logic we formalize the logic of actual obligation only. Therefore, the expression $O(B/C)$, for example, refers to an actual obligation. We are now in a position to answer van Fraassen's question: "if one knows that the actual outcome must satisfy C, and that $O(B/C)$ is true, ought one to follows a course of action leading to an outcome that satisfies B?" In light of the preceding remarks the answer is obviously "yes, surely, this is what obligations are about." That John need not follow a course of action leading to his marriage with Suzy, given that he killed her, only shows that we have no obligation to fulfill our prima facie obligations. Thus the principle of detachment in deontic logic is vindicated.

Given van Fraassen's confusion between prima facie and actual ought-statements in the John and Suzy paradox, the question of detachment acquires for him a new urgency. Consider Sartre's paradox where $O(A/C_1)$ and $O(\sim A/C_2)$ represent the conflicting prima facie ought-statements. Suppose we admit them inadvertently within the scope of van Fraassen's logic. $O(A/C_1)$ and $O(\sim A/C_2)$ do not constitute together a counter-example to AC2, the conditional version of (A1). On the other hand, if van Fraassen permits detachment in his logic, he will end up with OA and O~A which are represented in his system as $O(A/B\rightarrow B)$ and $O(\sim A/B\rightarrow B)$.[55] The conjunction of the last two ought-statements does constitute a counter-example to AC2. Therefore, to avoid the formulation of Sartre's paradox, van Fraassen rejects detachment in the quotation above.

The correct method for resolving Sartre's paradox in van Fraassen's system is the one we proposed. By distinguishing between prima facie and actual ought-statements, we reveal the conflicting ought-statements as prima facie and not actual obligation, as evidenced by (A1), the conflicting ought-statements do not fall within its scope. Consequently, Sartre's paradox cannot be formulated in his logic.

Furthermore, the principle of detachment is preserved under such a distinction. In the case of actual ought-statements, there is no argument against this principle. In the case of prima facie ought-statements, it leads to conflicting ought-statements; but that is acceptable in such a logic since (A1) is not an axiom there.

b. Hintikka's Solution. Hintikka also is aware that many ought-statements are conditional. He expresses this fact by the use of material implication in the formulation of such ought-statements in his logic. Furthermore, Hintikka is aware of the fact that "our commonplace notion of commitment is intrinsically ambiguous."[56] Consequently, he distinguishes between two important senses of commitment: the first concerns prima facie ought-statements, and the second concerns actual ought-statements. To this extent, Hintikka is in agreement with our analysis.

The distinction between prima facie and actual ought-statements is used by Hintikka to resolve the Conflict-of-Duty paradox, in the following manner: Given any ought-statement, he proposes one of two forms for expressing it in his logic. The first form, $O(A \rightarrow B)$ is used when the ought-statement being considered is a prima facie ought-statement. He observes that in this case, from $O(A \rightarrow B)$ "together with a factual statement no unconditional statement follows. For instance, A and $O(A \rightarrow B)$ do not imply OB."[57] Consequently, this form prevents the detachment of OB from its condition A, and the Conflict-of-Duty paradox cannot be formulated in this case. The second form, $A \rightarrow OB$, is used to express actual ought-statements. This form preserves our intuitions about detachment, and detachment in this case does not lead to paradoxes.[58]

Given the distinction between prima facie and actual ought-statements, Hintikka should not be worried about detachment in the case of prima facie ought-statement. As we argued earlier, their conflict does not constitute a counter-example to (A1), because such statements are only presumptions and do not fall within the scope of deontic logic. Hence, we do not need a non-detachable form for expressing prima facie ought-statements.

But Hintikka's understanding of prima facie ought-statements differs substantially from that of Sir David Ross, whom Hintikka describes as the one "who more than anyone else has been instrumental in introducing the concept of prima facie duty (obligation) into contemporary moral philosophy."[59] It also differs substantially from our understanding of that notion, as can be seen from the preceding sections. For Hintikka, a prima facie obligation is a kind of obligation. It is defined as an obligation which cannot be overruled in a deontically perfect world.[60] Consequently, the conflict of prima facie ought-statements does constitute for him a counter-example to (A1). Hence, Hintikka expresses such statements in a form that does not permit detachment.

It is clear from Hintikka's definition of prima facie obligation that his notion has very little to do with ours or Ross'. According to both of us, a prima facie ought-statement is overruled because considerations of the total situation rebut rather than confirm it. Therefore, a prima facie ought-statement can be overruled in a deontically perfect but complex world as much as it could be in any other. But according to Hintikka this is not the case. We now present the following example to illustrate the unintuitiveness of Hintikka's defintion.

Consider the case of a person who is living in a deontically perfect world. He goes to water the plants in his yard, as he ought to in a deontically perfect world, only to find out that his child has already watered the plants, as the child may in a deontically perfect world. Since overwatering the plants can harm them, the person concludes that he is no longer under an obligation to water them. On the contrary, he ought not to. His original prima facie obligation, therefore, has been overruled.

The notion of a deontically perfect world is not

a perfectly clear notion as Hintikka himself remarks.[61] Nevertheless, if we are to rely on our intutitions, the world described above is in accordance with these intuitions as to what a deontically perfect world is like. Our definition of prima facie obligation preserves these intuitions. But Hintikka's definition clashes with them. According to his definition the world described above is deontically imperfect.

As we saw at the beginning of this discussion, Hintikka's solution of the Conflict-of-Duty paradox is based on his understanding of prima facie and actual ought-statements. This understanding together with his wish to avoid the Conflict-of-Duty paradox led him to suggest a different logical form for each statement. Since we find his understanding of prima facie and actual ought-statements unacceptable, we find his argument for giving each statement a different logical form unacceptable insofar as it rests on this understanding.

Furthermore, in our discussion of the paradox of the Contrary-to-Duty Imperative in Chapter IV, we show that neither logical form of the two suggested by Hintikka above averts that paradox, which is a special case of this one.

c. von Wright's Solution. It is important in this discussion to note von Wright's later stance on the questions of conflict of duties and the validity of (A1) as a deontic principle. As we stated in the Introduction von Wright introduced in 1951 a system of deontic logic incorporating all but one of the axioms of what we now refer to as standard deontic logic. (A1) was among those axioms proposed by von Wright then.

When Chisholm's article "Contrary-to-Duty Imperatives and Deontic Logic" appeared in 1963, von Wright found it necessary to modify his system in order to handle the problems raised in Chisholm's article concerning conditional obligation. He introduced in 1964 "A New System of Deontic Logic" in which a new operator O(/) was introduced to assist in capturing that notion. Von Wright's original axioms

(A1) and (A2) were modified. The new versions were
conditionalized, but the deontic principle involved
in each case was preserved; so were the rules of
inference. But a new axiom pertaining to the logic
of the conditions of an obligation, called (B3) was
added:

(B3) $O(A/B \vee C) \leftrightarrow [O(A/B) \wedge O(A/C)]$.

Von Wright's New System did not fare very well.
It was possible to deduce from his system this
unpalatable theorem:

$O(A/C) \rightarrow O(A/C \wedge \sim B)$

which our discussion earlier has shown to be false.
It was also possible to deduce:

$\vdash O(A/B) \rightarrow \sim O(\sim A/C)$.

The first objection was raised recently by van
Fraassen.[62] The second was raised earlier by Geach
and accepted by von Wright.[63] Consequently, "A
Correction to a New System of Deontic Logic," appeared
in 1965. In this new attempt von Wright blamed his
problem on (A1) and its underlying principle. He
stated that:

> According to this [New] system a
> (genuine) conflict of duties was
> therefore a logical impossibility.
> This it obviously is not. One thing
> which the derivation of the absurdity
> in Section XII shows, is the necessity
> of allowing for the possibility of
> conflicting duties in a sane system
> of conditional norms.[64]

The absurdity referred to above is the one found
by Geach and mentioned earlier. In the derivation of
that absurdity not only (B1), the conditional version
of (A1) was used, but also (B3). Von Wright could
have corrected his system by rejecting (B3) rather than
(B1). Such a move would have been preferable since it
would have eliminated as well and in one stroke the

absurdity deduced later by van Fraassen. In the latter case, (B3) but not (B1) was involved in the deduction of the unacceptable result.

In his article, "An Analysis of Some Deontic Logics," Hansson observes that (B3) has some counter-intuitive consequences.[65] He produces two counter-examples to (B3). Here is one of them:

> Let the circumstance be that someone tries to save somebody from drowning. He has succeeded in landing the man. If the man is unconscious he is obligated to give him artificial respiration, but if the man is dead he is not. Since only one of O(A/B) and O(A/C) is true, it cannot be true that O(A/B∨C) i.e., if the man is dead or unconscious (and one does not know which) there is no obligation to give him artificial respiration.

It is worth noting that all these undesirable consequences of (B3) involve only this part of it:

(B3.1) $O(A/B \vee C) \rightarrow [O(A/B) \wedge O(A/C)]$.

No objections have been raised about the other part.

Since von Wright's basic argument for the rejection of (B1) rests on the derivability of absurdities in his New System which contains (B1), and since we have shown that all these absurdities involve (B3) in their derivation, while only one involves (B1) as well as (B3), it stands to reason that the source of the problem lies in (B3) and not (B1). Von Wright did not need to reject (B1), the conditional counterpart of (A1), in order to save his system. In light of all the absurdities and their derivations, and in light of the counterintuitiveness of (B3), von Wright should have rejected (B3) instead. His rejection of (B1) is thus not justified. Consequently, his solution to the second group of paradoxes, by accepting them as non-paradoxical given his rejection of (B1), is unacceptable. It does not rest on a good argument for rejecting (B3).[66]

   d. Segerberg's Solution. Segerberg devised a logic of commitment and obligation which turned out to have at least one counter-intuitive result.[67] Åqvist pointed out to Segerberg that the latter's logic validates the following theorem:

A com C→(A∧B)com C

i.e., if A commits the agent to C then (A∧B) commits him to C. "A commits the agent to B" can be expressed as "if A then the agent is commited to B," where "committed" is used in the sense of "obligated" and the "if-then" cannot be identified with material implication.[68] Åqvist showed that the theorem generates the Conflict-of-Duty paradox. This fact should be obvious by now from our discussion in Section 7.

   Segerberg recognized the strength of Åqvist's objection, but he dismissed it by offering his own solution to the Conflict-of-Duty paradox. He argued that "at least one of the com-operators in Åqvist's example is of a kind which our semantics does not formalize."[69] In light of our earlier discussion,[70] this remark is accurate. Segerberg then proceeded to dub the notion captured by the com-operator in his system as "strong commitment." He dubbed the one captured by Åqvist's example, as "weak commitment." He was then tempted to identify those two notions with the notions of prima facie and actual obligation.[71]

   The problem with Segerberg's position is that while it correctly resolves the Conflict-of-Duty paradox, it does not justify the counter-inutitive theorem mentioned above. Given an actual obligation C based on A, i.e., given that A commits the agent to C in the strong sense, then it does not follow, contrary to this theorem, that there is an actual obligation C based on (A∧B). Consider the example given in Section 8.b of this part. There, the actual obligation based on situation S was changed when C was added to the situation. This illustrates that the theorem is false even in cases where actual obligations alone are involved. The distinction introduced by

Segerberg does not help here.

The logic Segerberg captured in his system is that of universal obligation, i.e., an obligation which is true in every situation. Given such a notion of obligation, the above-mentioned theorem becomes true, and the logic becomes acceptable. But unfortunately, very few, if any, obligations are universal. As we showed in Section 7 of this part, obligations generally depend on the situation. Consequently, Segerberg's system captures the logic of very few obligations, if any. On the other hand, the logic of actual obligation captures the most common kind of obligation, i.e. that which depends on the situation. Furthermore, it captures also the logic of universal obligations since those are obligations that are actual in every situation. In light of these facts, Segerberg's system is not of great interest to us.

11. Some Concluding Remarks about Prima Facie and Actual Obligations.

The discussion above revealed a crucial difference between the logic of presumptions, or prima facie obligations and that of actual obligation. In the first case (A1) and the Kantian principle derivable from (A1) together with (A2.1) are both false. In the second case (A1), (A2.1) and the Kantian principle are all true. (A2.2) and the rules of inference hold for both. Consequently, we do know a lot about the logic of prima facie obligation. In such a logic not only (A2.2) and the rules of inference (R1)-(R4) hold but also either the usual definition of permission, i.e., $P = \sim O\sim$, or the usual assertion $\vdash OA \rightarrow PA$ will not hold. As we pointed out in Section II:3.b such a definition and assertion suffice to yield (A1) contrary to the assertion that prima facie oughts conflict.

Philosophers like Hintikka, Åqvist, and Castañeda regard what we have referred to as prima facie obligations or presumptions as obligations falling properly within the scope of deontic logic. Given such a view, our system of deontic logic should then consist of two fragments, one pertaining to the logic of prima facie obligation, another pertaining to the logic of actual obligation, together with some axioms connecting the two fragments. So far our discussion in this work has been informative as to the logic of both fragments and the connecting axioms. But our results except for those concerning actual obligation will remain informal since, as we argued in Section 2 of this part, presumptions do not fall within the scope of deontic logic.

We are now in a position to explain the confusion on which the claim that prima facie obligations are proper obligations falling within the scope of deontic logic partly rests. In discussing what we call prima facie obligations, philosophers have often had in mind a specific case of conflict as a paradigm.[72] This case was one where a situation, involving certain obligations, was changed by a new circumstance into another situation in which the initial obligations no longer hold. Such a case provides a complex example of prima facie obligations. We discussed it in Section 8.b. There we explained that an actual obligation based on an initial situation becomes a mere presumption when further circumstances are introduced.

Often, either the role of the circumstance or the role of the total situation in determining an obligation is ignored. When this happens, it becomes easy not to recognize the change of status an obligation undergoes when the situation changes. The change of the original obligation, from the status of an obligation in the old situation to the status of a presumption in the new one, goes undetected. In such a case philosophers continue to talk about two conflicting obligations without reference to the two different situations on the basis of which the two obligations were asserted; nor to the status of each obligation given one and the same situation.

In contrast to the paradigm case of conflict described above, the example we introduced in Section 2 describes one unchanged situation. It describes a hungry infant who is found in the park and who is allergic to milk. Since this example provides us with a simple case of prima facie obligations, our intuitions can be clearer in this instance. The prima facie obligation to feed the baby milk is readily exposed as a mere presumption in light of the totality of this unchanged situation.

The example mentioned above, as well as other examples which we presented in this chapter have also the advantage of clearing another confusion in the literature. Hintikka, Åqvist, Hansson and many others hold that a conflict of duties results from the violation of some obligation.[73] This is evident in Hintikka's definition of prima facie obligation which we discussed in Section 10.b. It is also evident in Åqvist's talk about "reparational obligation."[74] That this assumption is false should be obvious from our examples of conflict.

Footnotes

Chapter III

[1]Here is the proof for the thesis that (A2.1) holds if and only if (D) holds in a system containing propositional logic, (R3') and (DR1).

a. (i) That propositional logic, together (R3') and (D) implies (DR1) was shown on pp. 37-38. We now show that propositional logic together with (DR1) implies (A2.1).

(ii) $\vdash (A \wedge B) \rightarrow A$, and $\vdash (A \wedge B) \rightarrow B$ by propositional logic.
∴ $\vdash O(A \wedge B) \rightarrow OA$, $\vdash O(A \wedge B) \rightarrow OB$ by (DR1).
∴ $\vdash O(A \wedge B) \rightarrow (OA \wedge OB)$ by propositional logic.
Hence propositional logic and (DR1) imply (A2.1).
Q.E.D.

By (i) and (ii), we have shown that propositional logic, (R3') and (D) imply (A2.1).

b. Next, we show that propositional logic, (R3') and (A2.1) imply (DR1), and that propositional logic and (DR1) imply (D). But this was already shown in the proofs of (DR1) and clause (2) of theorem T_0 presented in Section II:1.d.

²See for example Dagfinn Føllesdal and Risto Hilpinen, "Deontic Logic: An Introduction," *Deontic Logic: Introductory and Systematic Readings*, ed. Risto Hilpinen, (New York: Humanities Press, 1971), 22.

³Harry Beatty, "On Evaluating Deontic Logics," *Journal of Philosophical Logic* 1 (1972), 441.

⁴Ibid.

⁵Ibid., 442.

⁶Ibid.

⁷Ibid.

⁸Bengt Hansson, "An Analysis of Some Deontic Logics," Hilpinen, 132.

⁹One proposal made by Hector-Neri Castañeda is based on the imperatival approach which will be evaluated in the last chapter of this work.

¹⁰Azizah al-Hibri Cox, "A Critical Survey in Deontic Logic," Master's thesis, (Detroit: Wayne State University, 1968) passim.

¹¹A. N. Prior, "Escapism: The Logical Basis of Ethics," *Essays in Moral Philosophy*, ed. A. I. Melden, (Seattle: University of Washington Press, 1958), 144.

¹²Ibid., 145.

¹³P. H. Nowell-Smith and E. J. Lemmon, "Escapism: The Logical Basis of Ethics," *Mind* 69 (1960), 293-294.

¹⁴Ibid., 295.

¹⁵See Cox, 13-14.

¹⁶H. P. Rickman, "Escapism: The Logical Basis of Ethics," *Mind* 72 (1963), 273-274. And John Robison, "Who, What, Where and When: A Note on Deontic Logic," *Philosophical Studies*, 15 (1964), 89-92.

¹⁷See Cox, 20-24.

¹⁸Lennart Åqvist, "Good Samaritans, Contrary-to-Duty Imperatives, and Epistemic Obligations," *Nous* 1 (1967), 371-378.

¹⁹See, for example, Castañeda, "Acts, the Logic

of Obligation, and Deontic Calculi," <u>Critica</u> 1 (1967), 79; and Bas van Fraassen's criticism of it in "The Logic of Conditional Obligation," <u>Journal of Philosophy</u> 1 (1972), 424.

[20] E. J. Lemmon, "Moral Dilemmas," <u>Philosophical Review</u> 71 (1962), 148. This paradox was introduced in Section II:5.f.

[21] Kurt Baier, <u>The Moral Point of View</u>, (New York: Random House, 1966), 38-50, and Castañeda, "A Theory of Morality," <u>Philosophy and Phenomenological Research</u> 17 (1957), passim. A more recent version of the criticism directed at Castañeda's proposal appears in my article "Castañeda's Theory of Morality." <u>Philosophy and Phenomenalogical Research</u>, forthcoming.

[22] W. David Ross, <u>Foundations of Ethics</u> (Oxford: The Clarendon Press, 1939), esp. 84-86. Also, <u>The Right and the Good</u> (Oxford: The Clarendon Press, 1930) esp. 18-20. Note that an ought-statement expresses an obligation.

[23] Ross, <u>Foundation of Ethics</u>, 85.

[24] Ibid., 86. Also Ross, <u>The Right and the Good</u>, 28.

[25] Ross, <u>Foundations of Ethics</u>, 85. Note that "Joe ought to do his work" is translated into our terminology as "it ought to be the case that Joe does his work." The act described in the first statement corresponds to the state of affairs in the second one.

[26] Baier, 38.

[27] Ross, <u>The Right and The Good</u>, 20.

[28] Lemmon, 148.

[29] Lemmon, "Deontic Logic and the Logic of Imperatives," <u>Logique et Analyse</u>, 29 (1965), 47.

[30] Lemmon, "Moral Dilemmas," 151.

[31] Lemmon, "Deontic Logic," 48.

[32] Ibid., 45.

[33] R. M. Hare, <u>Freedom and Reason</u> (Oxford: The Clarendon Press, 1963), 52.

[34] Ibid.

[35] Castañeda, "A Theory of Morality," 343.

[36] Ibid., 344.

[37] Ibid., 349.

[38] Ibid., 346.

[39] Ibid., 348-349.

[40] Ibid., 351.

[41] John Stuart Mill, *Utilitarianism*, (New York: E. P. Dutton & Co., 1910), 23.

[42] Hare, p. 38.

[43] See p. 92 of this work.

[44] W. J. Rees, "Moral Rules and the Analysis of 'Ought'," *Philosophical Review* 62 (1953), 27.

[45] Ross, *The Right and the Good*, 19, 28.

[46] Ibid., 20.

[47] Ross, *Foundations of Ethics*, 86.

[48] It was introduced by Lawrence Powers in "Some Deontic Logicians," *Nous* 1 (1967), 385-386.

[49] Jean-Paul Sartre, *Existentialism and Humanism*, translated by Philip Mairet (London: Methuen & Co., 1948), 35-36.

[50] van Fraassen, "Conditional Obligation," 418.

[51] Ibid., 422.

[52] Ibid.

[53] Ibid.

[54] Ibid., 423.

[55] Ibid., 421.

[56] Jaakko Hintikka, "Some Main Problems of Deontic Logic," Hilpinen, 87.

[57] Ibid., 89.

[58] Ibid.

[59] Ibid., 92.

[60] Ibid., 90.

[61] Ibid., 93.

[62] van Fraassen, "Conditional Obligation," 419.

[63] von Wright, "A New System of Deontic Logic," Hilpinen, 116.

[64] Ibid., 118.

[65] Hansson, 140.

[66] Hansson agrees with our conclusion, ibid.

[67] Krister Segerberg, "Some Logics of Commitment and Obligation," Hilpinen, 156.

[68] Ibid., 148.

[69] Ibid., 157.

[70] See Section B.2.

[71] Segerberg, 157.

[72] See for example Hintikka's example, 90. Also, Powers' example, 385.

[73] Hansson, 143.

[74] Åqvist, 371.

CHAPTER IV

A RESOLUTION OF THE LAST GROUP OF PARADOXES

1. A Study of the Contrary-to-Duty Imperative Paradox.

This paradox which was introduced in Section II:5.h represents a serious challenge to a deontic logic which accepts (Al). It specifies a situation in which one circumstance and three ought-statements are true. As explained in Section II:5.h, formalizing the four premises in the usual way results either in a conflict of duties or in a false deontic principle involving violated obligations. We now list again the four premises:

(1) Jones robs Smith.
(2) Jones ought not to rob Smith.
(3) It ought to be the case that if Jones does not rob Smith, he is not punished.
(4) If Jones robs Smith, then he ought to be punished.

The exact details of the problem of providing an adquate representation of all these four premises were discussed in Section II:5.h.

In light of the subsequent discussion in Chapter III, the possibility of representing (3) as $O(\sim A \rightarrow \sim B)$, and (4) as $A \rightarrow OB$, might be worth reconsidering. Originally these representations were rejected on the basis that together with the other premises they yielded:

(5) It ought to be the case that Jones is punished.

and

(6) It ought to be the case that Jones is not punished.

That is, they produced a case of conflict of duty. It is therefore advisable to reexamine this alternative representation in light of our distinction between prima facie and actual ought-statements. If we can show that any of the ought-statements in the paradox is a prima facie ought-statement, the conflict can then be resolved in the usual manner.

Unfortunately, this approach for resolving the paradox fails. Statement (2) is an instance of a moral principle which ranks high in our ethical hierarchy. As such (2) is usually true in deontic situations, unless there are extenuating circumstances of the sort discussed in Section III:B:7. Such circumstances are clearly absent in this example. The same is true of ought-statements (3) and (4). Furthermore, consideration of the situation as a whole as described by (1)-(4) does not reveal a tension among the four premises. Hence, all premises turn out as true even when global considerations are introduced.

The thrust of this paradox resides in the fact that all four premises are indeed consistent and represent a possible deontic situation even for someone who accepts (A1).[1] But when the premises are represented in a formal system in the usual ways, an unacceptable result is obtained. Therefore, this paradox raises the following question for philosophers who accept (A1) and the consistency of the premises: How can one represent (3) and (4) in a way that avoids the paradox and preserves our deontic principles?

2. Proposed Solutions to this Paradox.

In light of the discussion in Section III:B:10, we are already familiar with most of the salient proposals for solving this paradox. In this section, we evaluate these solutions. Since the solutions proposed by van Fraassen and Hansson are very similar to von Wright's solution, they will be discussed along with it.

a. Hintikka's Solution. As we explained in Section III:B:10.b, Hintikka suggested as a way out that a conditional ought-statement can have two alternative representations corresponding to the following two forms: $A \rightarrow OB$ and $O(A \rightarrow B)$. The second alternative is to be used in cases where detachment leads to problems like the one we are considering.[2] Given our version of the paradox of the Contrary-to-Duty Imperative, we already know that the first suggested form as well as the second fails in solving this paradox. This failure was exhibited in detail in Section II:5.h. Therefore, Hintikka's two alternative logical forms, contrary to his claim, do not resolve this paradox.[3] His solution fails.

b. Åqvist's Solution. In his "Good Samaritans, Contrary-to-Duty Imperatives, and Epistemic Obligations," Åqvist introduces a modified version of Hintikka's system.[4] Rather than have one kind of deontic operator O, Åqvist introduces an infinite number of deontic operators $O_1, O_2, O_3, \ldots$ obeying the usual rules. The first operator is to be used for expressing primary obligations, the second is to be used for secondary or reparational obligations incurred by violating primary obligations. When a reparational obligation itself is violated a new obligation is incurred; O_3 is used for expressing this new obligation; and so on.[5]

This approach renders the solution to the paradox of the Contrary-to-Duty Imperative extremely easy. The paradox can now be represented as:

(1) A
(2) $O_1 \sim A$
(3) $O_1(\sim A \rightarrow \sim B)$
(4) $A \rightarrow O_2 B$

Since Åqvist's system includes (DR1),[6] we obtain from the premises above by propositional logic:

(5) $O_1 \sim B$

and

(6) $O_2 B$

The contradiction disappears.

But this solution gives rise to another problem related to Contrary-to-Duty Imperatives. This problem was first noted by Powers.[7] Suppose that John violates the following two primary obligations.

O_1 (John does not get Suzy pregnant)
O_2^1 (John does not shoot Suzy).

By violating these primary obligations, the following two assertions become true:

O_2 (John marries Suzy)
$\sim O_2$ (John marries Suzy).

We have thus reconstructed a paradox similar to Plato's paradox, i.e., a paradox of conflict of duties whose resolution is intuitively obvious. But with the help of our distinction between prima facie and actual obligations this paradox can be resolved in the following manner. Considerations of the situation above as a whole reveal that the obligation to marry Suzy is not an actual obligation. It is only a prima facie obligation which is rebutted when the fact that Suzy is dead is introduced. Furthermore, since (A1) is a theorem of Åqvist's system for each O_i, it is fair to assume that Åqvist has formulated a logic of actual obligation. Consequently, the prima facie ought-statement O_2 (John marries Suzy) falls outside the scope of Åqvist's logic. This resolves the paradox.

Although the distinction between prima facie and actual obligations, together with Åqvist's distinction between primary and secondary obligations resolves the paradox of the Contrary-to-Duty Imperative, it does not resolve other versions of the Conflict-of-Duty paradox. We now construct a paradox in Åqvist's system which, unlike the previous one, cannot be resolved by resorting to the distinction between prima facie and actual obligation. This paradox represents a serious challenge to Åqvist's logic.

Consider the case of a child, Jimmy, who is on an outing with his parents. They take him to a private club. According to the rules of the club, children may not play with the slot machine. Hence, Jimmy's parents tell him that it ought to be the case that he does not play with the slot machine.

Let A stand for "Jimmy plays with the slot machine." We now have

(7) $O_1 \sim A$.

But Jimmy cannot resist the slot machine. He plays with it, i.e.,

(8) A.

This violates his primary obligation, expressed by (7). The parents are very distressed by Jimmy's behavior. They take him aside and have a long talk with him about the consequences of his disobedient behavior. Jimmy recognizes that he did something wrong. To make up for his bad behavior he promises not to play with the machine again. So now we have,

(9) $O_2 \sim A$.

The paradox can now be obtained by noting that the following rule is part of Åqvist's logic,[8]

If A, B are purely truth-functional formulae and $\vdash (B \leftrightarrow \sim A)$, then $\vdash (O_1 A \wedge B) \rightarrow O_2 B$.

In the example above, it is clear that A and $\sim A$ are purely truth-functional. Furthermore, by propositional logic, $\vdash (A \leftrightarrow \sim \sim A)$.[9] Hence, it follows from (7) and (8), that

(10) $O_2 A$.

But (9) and (10) contradict the fact that Åqvist's system contains the axiom (A1) for each O_i.[10] This new paradox in Åqvist's system cannot be removed from it by introducing the distinction between prima facie and actual obligations. We constructed the paradox on the basis of one actual primary obligation which yielded together with the violation of that obligation and Åqvist's logic, two actual secondary obligations that conflict. Therefore, we conclude that this paradox represents a serious challenge to Åqvist's logic. The logic succeeded in resolving the paradox of the Contrary-to-Duty Imperative, only to lead us into this other paradox.

c. Von Wright's Solution. As we have said in Section I:1, this paradox forced von Wright to modify his Old System and replace it with a New System of deontic logic. The new system contained a new operator O(/) to capture the notion of conditionality present in deontic statements of type (3) and (4). The failure of the usual modes of representation already indicated very clearly the failure of material implication or even strict implication[11] in handling this notion of conditionality. This necessitated the introduction of a richer notion of conditionality represented in von Wright's system by O(/).

The deontic operator O(/) supplied new representations of (3) and (4). In a representation of the form O(B/A), A stated the condition of the obligation. But unfortunately, von Wright's New System had two kinds of problems. The first kind we discussed at length in the previous section. It consisted in the fact that various contradictions and other unacceptable results are deducible from the system. The other lies in the fact that von Wright's sytem did not contain a rule for detaching ought-statements from their conditions. This, besides being counter-intuitive, as Hintikka points out, also violates adequacy criterion (a.2).[12] von Wright's later solution, where he denies (A1) altogether, is unacceptable for the reasons given in the previous section.

Van Fraassen's solution as supplied by his logic of conditional obligation is basically the same.[13] He uses the O(/) to capture the new notion of conditionality involved in the deontic statements (3) and (4). He also prohibits detachment, as we saw earlier. Consequently, we reject his solution as well. In the conclusion, we show that van Fraassen's system, like von Wright's is unacceptable.

Hansson's solution is very sketchy. Hansson simply endorses von Wright's introduction of the new operator O(/) as the way to resolve the paradox.[14] Examining his system we find no rule for detachment. Hence, the same criticism directed against von Wright and van Fraassen applies here. In the conclusion, we show some other problems in his system.

    d. Mott's Solution. Mott has very clear understanding of the full dimensions of this problem. As a result he presents a system of conditional deontic logic which he calls SDLC.[15] This new system combines the deontic operator O together with an operator □→ which represents according to Mott this stronger notion of conditionality,[16] to resolve Chisholm's paradox. The premises are now represented as:

(1') A
(2') O∼A
(3') ∼A□→O∼B
(4') A→OB.

Unlike von Wright and van Fraassen, Mott allows detachment in his system by introducing the following axiom:[17]

(A□→B)→(A→B).

So that we can derive from (3'), the following:

(3") ∼A→O∼B.

But since we have only O∼A and not ∼A, we cannot detach to get O∼B and regenerate the paradox.

    Mott does not explain why his new notion of conditionality extends only to (3'); but he does make one remark in this respect. He says that "we are quite at liberty to assume that behind the material conditional [A→OB] there lurks another 'moral principle' similar to [(3')]."[18] He then points out that his detachment axiom allows us to deduce (4') from this "moral principle." If this is the case, then such a "moral principle" will have the following form, if the detachment axiom is to yield (4'):

(4") A□→OB.

Stated in English (4") says that "if Jones does rob Smith then he ought to be punished," where the "if-then" expresses the stronger sense of conditionality here. But this reading is precisely (4). Hence, the English reading of (4') and (4") are the same. Mott has no adequate reason to assume that the stronger notion of conditionality involved in (3) is not also involved in (4); even though the involvement of that notion in only one of the premises suffices to resolve the paradox. Rather than argue that a "moral principle" involving the stronger notion of conditionality "lurks" behind (4), he should have simply pointed out that at least (3) involves that notion of conditionality and that perhaps (4) involves that notion too.

The reader might wonder further about the accuracy of Mott's representations. The English statement (3) is different from (4) in that the scope of O governs only the consequent in (4). Yet, in Mott's representation the scope of O was limited only to the consequent in both cases. But this objection can be met by pointing out to the ambiguity of the scope of O in English sentences. We discussed this ambiguity in Section III:A:6. Hintikka also asserts this ambiguity when he suggests that an ought-statement may have one of two logical forms, one with a wide scope for O, the other with a restricted scope. In discussing Chisholm's paradox, Hansson also entertained the idea that (3) and (4) "are in a sense parallel; it is a mere coincidence that 'ought' appears in the middle of [(4)] but at the beginning of [(3)]."[19] All this goes to show that we are on unsure ground as to the scope of O when representing a given English ought-statement. Further considerations are often useful in determining the correct scope of O.

If it is not intuitively clear upon reflection that the scope of O in (3) is limited, formal consideration can easily decide the matter. An interpretation which gives the O in (3) the wide scope results in a contradiction in Mott's system. Hence, it cannot be the correct representation of (3) in that system. The contradiction arises when we represent (3) as:

$O(\sim A \square \rightarrow \sim B)$.

By the rule (DR1) and the axiom that $(A\Box \to B) \to (A \to B)$, both of which are in Mott's system, we get:

$O{\sim}A \to O{\sim}B$

which constitutes together with (1), (2) and (4) an inconsistent set contrary to adequacy criterion (a.1).[20] Therefore, this representation of (3) is ruled out. The ambiguity of the scope of O is resolved rightly by Mott, in favor of the narrower one.

    Mott's solution meets the criteria of adequacy listed in Section II:5.h. Hence his solution is basically acceptable, although as we show in Chapter V:1.h the system as a whole is unacceptable.

3. Solution to the Paradox.

    Like Mott, von Wright, van Fraassen and Hansson, we recognize that a new notion is involved in Chisholm's paradox. We recognize that statements like (3) and (4) cannot be represented consistently solely by using the deontic operator O and material implication. But we differ from any of them in that while it seems reasonable to assume that such a notion is that of conditionality, the evidence at hand is sufficient for only a more modest conclusion - namely that the new notion involved is that of conditional obligation. Whether this notion is complex and is constituted of two simpler notions, an O and a /, as it were, remains to be investigated further. Consequently, in our solution to this paradox, we introduce the operator O(/), which replaces O, as a primitive deontic operator of conditional obligation.

    This operator rests solidly not only on the lessons of Chisholm's paradox, but also on the results in Chapter III which showed the basic dependence of obligations on conditions. Therefore, this new operator fits very nicely within the total framework of our earlier results. Chisholm's paradox itself is then solved in our system along Mott's line.

Footnotes

Chapter IV

[1] Peter L. Mott, "On Chisholm's Paradox," Journal of Philosophical Logic 2 (1973), 197.

[2] Jaakko Hintikka, "Some Main Problems of Deontic Logic," Deontic Logic: Introductory and Systematic Readings, ed. Risto Hilpinen, (New York: Humanities Press, 1971), 89.

[3] Ibid., 89.

[4] Lennart Åqvist, "Good Samaritans, Contrary-to-Duty Imperatives, and Epistemic Obligations." Nous 1(1967), 361-379.

[5] Ibid., 377.

[6] Ibid., 365.

[7] Lawrence Powers, "Some Deontic Logicians," Nous 1 (1967), 386. Note that my perception of this problem in the discussion above differs from that of Powers.

[8] Ibid., 373.

[9] Propositional logic is included in Åqvist's deontic logic. Ibid., 362.

[10] Ibid.

[11] Mott, 206.

[12] Hintikka, 89. Also see p. 40 of this work for adequacy criterion (a.2).

[13] Bas van Fraassen, "The Logic of Conditional Obligation," Journal of Philosophical Logic 1 (1972), 417-438.

[14] Bengt Hansson, "An Analysis of Some Deontic Logics," Hilpinen, 133.

[15] Mott, 207-210

[16] Ibid., 208.

[17] Ibid.

[18] Ibid., 209.

[19] Hansson, 133.
[20] See p. 40 of this work.

CHAPTER V

THE LOGICAL SYSTEM S

1. The Foundation of S.

The totality of discussion, exposition, and criticism preceding this part has been directed at determining the principles of a deontic logic which capture our deontic intuitions and does not lead us into paradoxes. In the earlier chapters we agreed that all of the principles on which SDL⁻ is based are worth preserving. We showed that these principles do not lead to paradoxes. In doing that we examined the major paradoxes of deontic logic and showed what the real problems were. The last paradox to be discussed represented a serious challenge to SDL⁻. It showed that the language of SDL⁻ is not rich enough to express an important kind of deontic statements--the contrary-to duty imperatives. Our system S will preserve the basic principles on which SDL⁻ rests, but will supercede SDL⁻ by supplying a richer system which is capable of handling Chisholm's paradox. It will also include a fundamental deontic principle not suggested originally by von Wright, namely, the principle of detachment. In Sections II:10.a-b, we defended this principle at length, and argued that the suspicions surrounding it are based on a confusion. Our task now is to present this system in full as the standard deontic system S, which succeeds in capturing our deontic intuitions.

The semantics we shall choose for S is based on the notion of possible worlds. As we stated in the introduction, the truth of an ought-statement at a world α is defined in terms of a certain set of possible worlds. The exact definition appears in Section 5.d. These worlds can thus be viewed as participants in providing the moral standard for world α.

The notion of 'possible worlds' has often been regarded with suspicion.[1] Hence it might seem inadvisable to base our semantics on this notion. But we regard such suspicions as unfounded. Our view on the matter coincides with that of David Lewis who argues convincingly against such suspicions in Counterfactuals.[2] Consequently, we have no scruples in basing our semantics on the notion of 'possible worlds'.

We shall now present our system S. This system provides the basis for various deontic logics. It can be enhanced in many ways to capture more of our deontic intuitions. To emphasize this fact we shall propose one such enhancement of S, the system S' based on S and which contains several additional axioms.

Furthermore, we shall consider alternative semantics to S. We shall also compare S with other systems proposed in the literature. Such studies will reveal further the virtues of S. Finally, we shall suggest several ways in which S can be further enhanced. The development of these possibilities will be left for future research.

2. The Syntax of S.

The language of S consists of

a. Atomic sentences: $\mathbb{P}_0, \mathbb{P}_1, \mathbb{P}_2, \ldots$.
b. One nullary operation: $\perp$.
c. Parentheses: (,), [,].
c. Two binary operations: $\rightarrow$, $O(/)$.

The set of atomic sentences is denumerable. $\perp$ represents falsity, $\rightarrow$ represents material implication, while $O(/)$ represents conditional obligation. The other familiar operations, like $\sim$ (negation), $\vee$ (disjunction), $\wedge$ (conjunction) and $\leftrightarrow$ (biconditionality), are definable in terms of the given operations.[3]

Finally, we follow von Wright and others in defining the familiar monadic operator O, by $OA = O(A/T)$.[4]

3. Axiom Schemas and Rules of Inference for S.

The system S will consist of the following axiom

schemas and rules of inference

A1. ⊢ A, where A is a tautology.
A2. ⊢ ~O(⊥/C).

This axiom asserts the Kantian principle "ought" implies "can" which we defended at several places in this work. It says that under no circumstances is the impossible obligatory. This raises the question of whether the impossible is not obligatory under impossible circumstances. Our intuitions on this point are not clear.[5] For formal considerations, we choose to answer the question in this system by asserting that the impossible is never obligatory even under impossible circumstances. Later, we show how a richer system can handle this problem more satisfactorily.

A3. ⊢ O(B/A)→(A→O(B/T)).

This axiom says that if something is obligatory under a certain condition, it is obligatory, if that condition obtains, under tautologous conditions. In light of the fact that we follow von Wright in defining the traditional monadic operator by OA = O(A/T), it follows that A3 is the axiom for detachment in S. The principle of detaching an obligation from its conditions was also defended in Chapter II.

A4. ⊢ [O(B/A)∧O(B/A')]→O(B/A∨A').

We shall call this axiom the axiom of dilemma. We regard this axiom, which was not discussed previously, as obvious. But readers who have in mind an example like this one might think otherwise. Consider the following situation. Suppose that a certain civil servant of a certain country, finds himself in a situation where the following two statements are true. First, if he marries the prime minister's daughter, then he ought to be rewarded. Second, if he marries the president's daughter, then he ought to be rewarded. To insure this reward the civil servant marries both daughters. He reasons that in the new situation $C_1 \vee C_2$ is certainly true, where C_1 stands for "he marries the prime minister's daughter" and C_2 stands

103

for "he marries the president's daughter". Therefore by the two statements above, the fact that $C_1 \vee C_2$ is true and by A4, it follows that he ought to be rewarded. We know on the other hand that such a conclusion is false.

But this example does not constitute a counter-example to A4. It is clear from the example that the two statements above express prima facie and not actual obligations. Each statement was asserted on the basis of one aspect of the situation and not on the basis of the situation as a whole. Therefore, this example shows that A4 is not acceptable as an axiom in the logic of prima facie obligation. On the other hand, in proposing S we are proposing a logic of obligation. We have already argued in Chapter III that prima facie obligations are not obligations. Consequently, the example given above does not constitute a counter-example to A4 in S.

A4 is an unexceptional axiom. It states that if it ought to be the case that B given A, and if it ought to be the case that B given A', then it ought to be the case that B given A or given A'. Explained in this manner the plausibility of A4 becomes obvious.

S has three rules of inference:

R0. $\dfrac{\vdash A \rightarrow B,\ \vdash A}{\vdash B}$ (Modus Ponens).

R1. $\dfrac{\vdash (A \wedge B) \rightarrow D}{\vdash [O(A/C) \wedge O(B/C)] \rightarrow O(D/C)}$.

This rule expresses the conditional version of (A2.2) plus (DR1), the latter being the formal counterpart to principle P. Both (A2.2) and P were discussed in Chapter III.

R2. $\dfrac{\vdash A \leftrightarrow A'}{\vdash O(B/A) \leftrightarrow O(B/A')}$.

This is a rule of extensionality for circumstances. Its validity is immediately obvious.

This concludes the axiom schemas and rules of inference of S. We note that A1 and R0 insure that propositional logic is included in S.⁶ Before going into the semantics of S, we would like to make the reader more familiar with S by exhibiting two derived rules and a theorem of S.

4. Some Derived Rules and a Theorem of S.

Derived Rule 1

$$\frac{\vdash A \rightarrow B}{\vdash O(A/C) \rightarrow O(B/C)} \cdot$$

This rule is the conditionalized version of (DR1) which is a derived rule in von Wright's Old System. (DR1) was introduced in Section I:1. This rule will be referred to as DR1 to distinguish it from (DR1).

To prove DR1, we assume that $\vdash A \rightarrow B$ and show that $\vdash O(A/C) \rightarrow O(B/C)$. By our assumption and propositional logic we derive $\vdash (A \wedge A) \rightarrow B$. By R1 we infer that $\vdash [O(A/C) \wedge O(A/C)] \rightarrow O(B/C)$. By propositional logic, it follows that $\vdash O(A/C) \rightarrow O(B/C)$. Q.E.D.

Derived Rule 2

$$\frac{\vdash A \leftrightarrow A'}{\vdash O(A/C) \leftrightarrow O(A'/C)} \cdot$$

We assume that $\vdash A \leftrightarrow A'$. By propositional logic, $\vdash A \rightarrow A'$ and $\vdash A' \rightarrow A$. Hence, by DR1 $\vdash O(A/C) \rightarrow O(A'/C)$ and $\vdash O(A'/C) \rightarrow O(A/C)$. Thus, $\vdash O(A/C) \leftrightarrow O(A'/C)$, by propositional logic. Q.E.D.

This rule is the conditionalized counterpart to (R3'), the rule which replaced (R3) in our version of von Wright's Old System. It will be referred to as DR2.

Theorem.

Each of (1)-(8) is a theorem.

(1) $[O(A/C) \wedge O(B/C)] \rightarrow O(A \wedge B/C)$.

(2) $O(A \wedge B/C) \rightarrow [O(A/C) \wedge O(B/C)]$.
(3) $[O(A \vee B/C) \wedge O(\sim B/C)] \rightarrow O(A/C)$.
(4) $\sim [O(A/C) \wedge O(\sim A/C)]$.
(5) $O(A/C) \rightarrow \sim O(\sim A/C)$.
(6) $(O(A/C) \wedge [O(A/T) \rightarrow O(B/T)]) \rightarrow (C \rightarrow O(B/T))$.
(7) $\sim O(\perp/T)$.
(8) $[O(A/B \vee C) \wedge O(A/\sim B \vee C)] \rightarrow O(A/C)$.

Some of these clauses deserve to be pointed out especially. (1) is the conditionalized version of (A2.2) introduced in Section I:3.c. (2) is the conditionalized version of (A2.1) introduced in the same section. Both (A2.1) and (A2.2) were incorporated in von Wright's Old System by one axiom (A2). (4) is the conditionalized version of (A1). Like (4) (5) expresses the important deontic principle that obligations do not conflict given the same condition. This principle was expressed in von Wright's Old System. It was later repudiated by him in his modified New System. This principle was defended at length in the second part of Chapter II.

Proof.

(1) By propositional logic $\vdash (A \wedge B) \rightarrow (A \wedge B)$. Hence we infer by R1 that $\vdash [O(A/C) \wedge O(B/C)] \rightarrow O(A \wedge B/C)$. Q.E.D.

(2) By propositional logic $\vdash (A \wedge B) \rightarrow A$. By (DR1) we infer that $\vdash O(A \wedge B/C) \rightarrow O(A/C)$. Again, by propositional logic $\vdash (A \wedge B) \rightarrow B$. Consequently by (DR1) $\vdash O(A \wedge B/C) \rightarrow O(B/C)$. The last two results yield by propositional logic that $\vdash O(A \wedge B/C) \rightarrow [O(A/C) \wedge O(B/C)]$. Q.E.D.

(3) $\vdash [(A \vee B) \wedge \sim B] \rightarrow A$ by propositional logic. Therefore, by (DR1) we infer that $\vdash O((A \vee B) \wedge \sim B/C) \rightarrow O(A/C)$. Furthermore, by clauses (1) and (2) of this theorem:

$\vdash O((A \vee B) \wedge \sim B/C) \leftrightarrow [O(A \vee B/C) \wedge O(\sim B/C)]$.

Hence by propositional logic $\vdash [O(A \vee B/C) \wedge O(\sim B/C)] \rightarrow O(A/C)$. Q.E.D.

(4) $\vdash \sim O(A \wedge \sim A/C)$ by A2; DR2 and propositional logic; hence, $\vdash \sim [O(A/C) \wedge O(\sim A/C)]$ by clause (1) of

this theorem. Q.E.D.

(5) This clause follows from (4) by propositional logic.

(6) By propositional logic
$\vdash [O(A/T) \land [O(A/T) \to O(B/T)]] \to O(B/T)$. Also by A3 and propositional logic $\vdash [O(A/C) \land C] \to O(A/T)$. Therefore by propositional logic

$\vdash [O(A/C) \land C \land [O(A/T) \to O(B/T)]] \to O(B/T)$.

That is, by propositional logic,

$\vdash [O(A/C) \land [O(A/T) \to O(B/T)] \land C] \to O(B/T)$,

which yields by propositional logic again that

$\vdash [O(A/C) \land [O(A/T) \to O(B/T)]] \to (C \to O(B/T))$. Q.E.D.

(7) This follows immediately from A2 which says:

$\vdash \sim O(\bot/C)$.

(8) By A4, $\vdash [O(A/B \lor C) \land O(A/\sim B \lor C)] \to O(A/(B \lor C) \lor (\sim B \lor C))$, i.e., by propositional logic, $\vdash [O(A/B \lor C) \land O(A/\sim B \lor C)] \to O(A/(B \lor \sim B) \lor C)$. Therefore by propositional logic and R2, $\vdash [O(A/B \lor C) \land O(A/\sim B \lor C)] \to O(A/C)$. Q.E.D.

The facts exhibited about S in the last two sections give us a better understanding of this system. We shall now describe other aspects of S.

5. Semantics for S.

a. A Model for S. We define a model for S as a triple, $m = \langle W, R, P \rangle$, in which W is a set called the domain of m, R a relation in $W \times \mathcal{P}(W) \times \mathcal{P}(W)$ and P is a mapping from the set N of natural numbers to $\mathcal{P}(W)$.

We may regard W as the set of possible worlds, R as a deontic relation which associates with each world α, and condition C, a set of worlds Y. We may regard the members of Y as deontic alternatives associated by R with a given world α and a given condition C. We shall discuss R further in the following section and in Section VII:2.

P_n is the set of possible worlds at which the atomic sentence $\mathbb{P}_h$, holds for each n.

b. Restrictions on R. The relation R satisfies the following restrictions for any $X, Y \subseteq W$, and for any $\alpha \in W$:

R.1 Not $R(\alpha,W,\varphi)$.
R.2 If $\alpha \in X$ and $R(\alpha,X,Y)$, then $R(\alpha,W,Y)$.
R.3 If $R(\alpha,X,Y)$ and $R(\alpha,X',Y')$, then $R(\alpha,X \cup X', Y \cup Y')$.
R.4 If $R(\alpha,X,Y)$ and $R(\alpha,X,Y')$, then $R(\alpha,X,Y \cap Y')$.

We note that in $R(\alpha,X,Y)$ the set of worlds Y is a set of deontic alternatives to α with respect to the set X which defines a particular condition of an obligation.

The first restriction rules out the possiblity that given a set X, a world α may have no deontic alternatives whatsoever, i.e., worlds where the obligations in α are satisfied. Clearly, the only case where an obligation cannot be satisfied in any world is the case where the obligation requires bringing about an impossible state of affairs. But such obligations were denied by our axiom A2. Therefore, our restriction validates A2 in S.

R.1 does not exclude the possibility that $X = \varphi$, i.e., that the condition of obligation is impossible. As we said earlier, our intuitions on this matter are unclear. In this system we choose to permit, for formal reasons, the possiblity that $X = \varphi$. In Chapter VII a suggestion will be made for eliminating this case in a richer system of deontic logic.

The second condition says that if α is a member of the set of worlds that define a condition with respect to which Y is a set of deontic alternatives to α, then Y is a set of deontic alternatives to α unconditionally.

To understand this restriction better we must note

that when considering $R(\alpha,X,Y)$, the set of worlds X which defines a certain condition turns out to be the set of all worlds in which that condition is satisfied. Consequently, since α is a member of this set of worlds, this condition is satisfied at α. Hence the set of deontic alternatives to α determined on the basis of the condition is the same as that determined unconditionally with respect to α, since the condition already holds at α. Introducing the condition as a separable factor in determining the set of deontic alternatives to α does not alter this result. Consequently, the condition can be dropped.

Therefore, if an obligation conditional upon C is true at α, and C is true at α, then it follows that the obligation is true at α unconditionally. Hence, this restriction validates A3 in S.

The third restriction says that if R associates a set of worlds Y with a world α on the basis of a condition C defined by X, and if it associates another set of worlds Y' with α on the basis of another condition C' defined by X', then given the set $X \cup X'$ defining the condition C-or-C', R associates with α the set of all worlds that are in the set $Y \cup Y'$. This explanation makes R3 a reasonable restriction. It also shows that this restriction validates A4 in S.

Finally, the fourth restriction says that if R associates a set of worlds Y with a world α on the basis of a condition defined by a set X, and associates as well another set Y' with α on the basis of the same condition defined by X, then R associates both Y and Y' with α on the basis of that condition defined by X. This restriction is intuitive and it validates R1.

c. Some Definitions. We now define the following abbreviations:

$\|A\|^m$ is the set of worlds in m at which A is true.

$\models_\alpha^m$ A means that the sentence A is true at the world α in the model m.

$\models^m A$ iff $\models^m_\alpha A$ for every α in m.

$\models A$ iff $\models^m_\alpha A$ for every model m.

d. The Notion of Truth at α in m. This notion is defined as follows:

(i) $\models^m_\alpha P_n$ iff $\alpha \in P_n$, for any n;

(ii) not $\models^m_\alpha$;

(iii) $\models^m_\alpha A \rightarrow B$ iff if $\models^m_\alpha A$ then $\models^m_\alpha B$;

(iv) $\models^m_\alpha O(A/C)$ iff there are sets X, Y $\subseteq$ W such that $R(\alpha,X,Y)$, $Y \subseteq \|A\|^m$ and $X = \|C\|^m$.

The last clause in this definition is unfamiliar. Therefore, we make a few remarks to explain it. Given a world α, "it ought to be the case that A, on condition C" is true in that world, according to clause (iv), if and only if A is true in every single world of some set of possible worlds associated by R with α on the basis of condition C. That R associates deontic alternatives with α, i.e., ones where all obligations in α are satisfied, is revealed partially by the requirement that A is true in every member of this set of worlds. This set of worlds can therefore be regarded as supplying a moral standard to world α with respect to condition C.

But not any world where A is true participates in supplying such a moral standard. Since some worlds in which A is true can be deontically different or even irrelevant to α, as we show in Section VI:B.2 we require that $Y \subseteq \|A\|^m$. This now reveals further the fact that the worlds associated by R with α are deontic alternatives.

Seen in light of the explanation above, clause (iv) becomes more intuitive.

e. Some Additional Definitions. S is defined as the smallest set of sentences generated by axioms A1-A4, and rules R0, R1 and R2.

A sentence A is defined as a theorem in S, i.e., $\vdash A$, just in case $A \in S$.

A is derivable in S from a set of sentences if and only if the set contains $A_1,\ldots,A_n$ ($n \geq 0$) such that $\vdash (A_1 \wedge \ldots \wedge A_n) \to A$. Where $n = 0$, we identify the conditional with the consequent.

A set of sentences is consistent in S just in case there is a sentence which is not S-derivable from it.

A set of sentences is maximal in S if and only if it is S-consistent and has no S-consistent extensions.

6. The Soundness of S.

We show now that S is a sound system, i.e., we show that if A is a theorem of S, then A is a valid sentence of S.

The Soundness Theorem for S.

For any sentence A in S, if $\vdash A$, then $\models A$.

Proof.

It is sufficient to show that axioms A1-A4 are valid and that R0, R1 and R2 preserve validity. That A1 is valid follows immediately from our definition of the notion of truth presented in Section 5.d above.[7] Also by clause (iii) of the definition of truth it is clear that R0 preserves validity.

a. A2 is Valid. We show the validity of every formula which has the shape $\sim\!O(\perp/C)$. Therefore, we need to show that $\models \sim\!O(\perp/C)$, i.e., that $\models_\alpha^m \sim\!O(\perp/C)$ for all models m of S and worlds α in m. Let m be any model, α any world and assume for reductio that not $\models_\alpha^m \sim\!O(\perp/C)$. Then $\models_\alpha^m O(\perp/C)$. It follows that there are sets $X, Y \subseteq W$ such that $R(\alpha,X,Y)$, $Y \subseteq \|\perp\|^m$ we know

111

that $\|\bot\|^m = \omega$. Hence by set theory $Y \subseteq \omega$, which means that $Y = \omega$. So it follows that $R(\alpha,X,\omega)$ contrary to R.1. Consequently, our assumption must be false. Therefore, for every model m and world α in m, $\models_\alpha^m \sim O(\;/C)$. That is, by definition of $\models$ in 6.c, $\models \sim O(\bot/C)$. Q.E.D.

b. A3 is Valid. We show the validity of every formula of the shape $O(B/A) \to (A \to O(B/T))$. Therefore we need to show that $\models O(B/A) \to (A \to O(B/T))$, i.e., $\models_\alpha^m O(B/A) \to (A \to O(B/T))$ for every model m and world α in W.

Let m be any model m for S and α any member of W. By the definition of truth, clause (iii), it is sufficient to show that if $\models_\alpha^m O(B/A)$ and $\models_\alpha^m A$ then $\models_\alpha^m O(B/T)$. So we assume that $\models_\alpha^m O(B/A)$ and $\models_\alpha^m A$.

By the first assumption that $\models_\alpha^m O(B/A)$ and the definition of truth, clause (iv), it follows that there are sets $X, Y \subseteq W$ such that $R(\alpha,X,Y)$, $Y \subseteq \|B\|^m$ and $X = \|A\|^m$. By the second assumption that $\models_\alpha^m A$ and the definition of $\|A\|^m$ together with the fact that $X = \|A\|^m$ given above, it follows that $\alpha \in X$. Therefore, by R.2, the fact that $R(\alpha,X,Y)$ mentioned above, and the fact that $\alpha \in X$ which we have just established, it follows that $R(\alpha,W,Y)$.

But $W = \|T\|^m$ by definition of these notions. Hence, there are sets $X, Y \subseteq W$ such that $R(\alpha,W,Y)$, $Y \subseteq \|B\|^m$ and $X = \|T\|^m$. By definition of truth, clause (iv), this yields that $\models_\alpha^m O(B/T)$. This establishes the desired result. Q.E.D.

c. A4 is Valid. We show the validity of every formula of the shape $[O(B/A) \land O(B/A')] \to O(B/A \lor A')$. Therefore we show that

$$\models [O(B/A) \land O(B/A')] \to O(B/A \lor A'),$$

which means by definition of $\models$ in Section 5.c that we have to show that for every model m for S, and for every α in W,

$\models^m_\alpha [O(B/A) \wedge O(B/A')] \to O(B/A \vee A')$.

Let m be any model for S and α any member of W. By definition of truth clause (iii), it is sufficient to show that if $\models^m_\alpha O(B/A) \wedge O(B/A')$, then $\models^m_\alpha O(B/A \vee A')$. Hence we assume that $\models^m_\alpha O(B/A) \wedge O(B/A')$ and show that $\models^m_\alpha O(B/A \vee A')$.

From our assumption, the definition of truth clauses (ii) and (iii), together with the definition of conjunction (and negation) given in footnote 3, it follows that:

$\models^m_\alpha O(B/A)$ and $\models^m_\alpha O(B/A')$.

$\models^m_\alpha O(B/A)$ yields by the definition of truth clause (iv), that there are sets $X, Y \subseteq W$ such that $R(\alpha,X,Y)$, $Y \subseteq \|B\|^m$ and $X = \|A\|^m$. Similarly, $\models^m_\alpha O(B/A')$ yields that there are propositions $X', Y' \subseteq W$ such that $R(\alpha,X',Y')$, $Y' \subseteq \|B\|^m$ and $X' = \|A'\|^m$.

By the third restriction on R we have $R(\alpha, X \cup X', Y \cup Y')$. Also since $Y \subseteq \|B\|^m$, $Y' \subseteq \|B\|^m$ then $Y \cup Y' \subseteq \|B\|^m$. Furthermore $X \cup X' = \|A\|^m \cup \|A'\|^m = \|A \vee A'\|^m$. Therefore, there are sets, namely $X \cup X'$ and $Y \cup Y'$ such that $R(\alpha, X \cup X', Y \cup Y')$, $Y \cup Y' \subseteq \|B\|^m$ and $X = \|A \vee A'\|^m$. Therefore by clause (iv) of the definition of truth $\models^m_\alpha O(B/A \vee A')$. This establishes that
$\models^m_\alpha [O(B/A) \wedge O(B/A')] \to O(B/A \vee A')$. But m was any model for S and α any member of W; hence by definition of $\models$ and the above

$\models^m_\alpha [O(B/A) \wedge O(B/A')] \to O(B/A \vee A')$. Q.E.D.

d. R1 Preserves Validity. We need to show that if $\models (A \wedge B) \to D$, then $\models [O(A/C) \wedge O(B/C)] \to O(D/C)$. This establishes the claim that R1 preserves validity. Therefore we assume that $\models (A \wedge B) \to D$ and show that $\models [O(A/C) \wedge O(B/C)] \to O(D/C)$. By definition of $\models$ and the truth definition, clause (iii), it is sufficient to show that if $\models^m_\alpha O(A/C) \wedge O(B/C)$ then $\models^m_\alpha O(D/C)$ for any model m and world α in W. So let m be any model, α any world, and assume that $\models^m_\alpha O(A/C) \wedge O(B/C)$. Hence

$\models^m_\alpha O(A/C)$ and $\models^m_\alpha O(B/C)$ by the truth definition. We need to show that $\models^m_\alpha O(D/C)$.

By our assumption that $\models^m_\alpha O(A/C)$, we get by the definition of truth, clause (iv), that there are sets X, $Y \subseteq W$ such that $R(\alpha,X,Y)$, $Y \subseteq \|A\|^m$ and $X = \|C\|^m$. Also by the assumption that $\models^m_\alpha O(B/C)$, we get similarly that there are sets X', $Y' \subseteq W$ such that $R(\alpha,X',Y')$, $Y' \subseteq \|B\|^m$ and $X' = \|C\|^m$. Hence, $X' = \|C\|^m = X$. Also, by the original assumption and the definition of $\models$, it follows that $\|A \wedge B\|^m \subseteq \|D\|^m$. But $\|A \wedge B\|^m = \|A\|^m \cap \|B\|^m$ by set theory. Hence $Y \cap Y' \subseteq \|D\|^m$. Furthermore we have $R(\alpha,X,Y)$ from above as well as $R(\alpha,X',Y')$. But since we know from above that $X = X'$, we also have $R(\alpha,X,Y')$. Therefore, by the fourth restriction on R, we have $R(\alpha,X,Y \cap Y')$. Consequently, there are sets, namely X and $Y \cap Y' \subseteq W$, such that $R(\alpha,X,Y \cap Y')$, $Y \cap Y' \subseteq \|D\|^m$ and $X = \|C\|^m$. Hence by definition of truth, clause (iv), we have that $\models^m_\alpha O(D/C)$. This establishes that,

$\models^m_\alpha [O(A/C) \wedge O(B/C)] \to O(D/C)$.

But m and α were any model and any member of W. Hence $\models [O(A/C) \wedge O(B/C)] \to O(D/C)$. This establishes the desired result.

e. R2 Preserves Validity. We need to show that if $\models A \leftrightarrow A'$, then $\models O(B/A) \leftrightarrow O(B/A')$. So we assume that $\models A \leftrightarrow A'$. To show $\models O(B/A) \leftrightarrow O(B/A')$, it is sufficient to show $\models^m_\alpha O(B/A) \leftrightarrow O(B/A')$ for every model m and every world α.

Let m be any model for S and α any member of W. We show that $\models^m_\alpha O(B/A) \leftrightarrow O(B/A')$ given the assumption above. By definition of the truth-functional connectives and the definition of truth, clause (iv), it is sufficient to show that $\models^m_\alpha O(B/A) \to O(B/A')$ and $\models^m_\alpha O(B/A') \to O(B/A)$. Let us show that $\models^m_\alpha O(B/A) \to O(B/A')$ only. The proof that $\models^m_\alpha O(B/A') \to O(B/A)$ is similar.

By definition of truth, clause (iii), it is sufficient to show that if $\models^m_\alpha O(B/A)$ then $\models^m_\alpha O(B/A')$.

So we assume that $\models^m_\alpha O(B/A)$ and show that $\models^m_\alpha O(B/A')$. By the definition of truth clause (iv) and the last assumption, it follows that there are sets $X, Y \subseteq W$ such that $R(\alpha,X,Y)$, $Y \subseteq \|B\|^m$ and $X = \|A\|^m$. But by our original assumption that $\models A \leftrightarrow A'$ and the definition of $\|A\|^m$ we know that $\|A\|^m = \|A'\|^m$. Therefore $X = \|A'\|^m$. This means by the definition of truth clause (iv) that $\models^m_\alpha O(B/A')$. This establishes that $\models^m_\alpha O(B/A) \rightarrow O(B/A')$. This establishes the desired result. Q.E.D.

    f. The Soundness of S has been Established. We have shown in parts a-e that every axiom schema is valid, and that every rule of S preserves validity. Consequently, every theorem of S is valid. Therefore S is sound. Q.E.D.

7. The Completeness of S.

A system is complete if and only if every valid sentence in the system is a theorem; i.e., for all A, if $\models A$ then $\vdash A$. In order to show that S is complete we introduce a particular model of S which we call the canonical model of S. The canonical model is of interest us because it has the characteristic that the true sentences in it are exactly the theorems of S.

    a. A Sketch of the Completeness Proof for S. As we know from Section 3, by axiom A1 and rule R0 of S, propositional logic is a fragment of S. Therefore, Lindenbaum's lemma, which holds of every logic that includes propositional logic, is applicable to S.[8]

Lindenbaum's Lemma.

Every S-consistent set of sentences has an S-maximal extension.

From this lemma, the following corollary follows:[9]

Corollary.

The theorems of S are just the sentences that belong to every S-maximal set of sentences.

Now if we can show of the canonical model $m = \langle W,R,P \rangle$ where W is defined as the set of all S-maximal sets, that

(1) for all α in W, if $\models^m_\alpha A$, then $A \in \alpha$.

Then given the corollary above which says that

(2) $\vdash A$ iff for all α in W, $A \in A$.

We can conclude that for a canonical model m,

(3) if $\models^m A$, then $\vdash A$,

by (1) and (2) above, and the definition of $\models^m$. It follows from (3) that

(4) If $\models A$, then $\vdash A$

since it follows from $\models A$ by definition of $\models$ that $\models^m A$, where m is our canonical model.

Hence this proof for the completeness of S rests on our ability to show (1), and to show that the canonical model is a model for S. We shall now, therefore, establish (1).

b. The Canonical Model m. Let $m = \langle W,R,P \rangle$, where W is the set of maximal sets of sentences, R a relation in $W \times P(W) \times P(W)$ and P a mapping from the set of natural numbers to $P(W)$; such that R and P are defined as follows:

$R(\alpha,W,Y)$ iff for some setnences A, B, $|A| = X$, $|B| \subseteq Y$ and $O(B/A) \in \alpha$

and

$P_n = |\mathbb{P}_n|$

where $|A|$ is defined as the class of all S-maximal sets of sentences in S containing the sentence A. This defines the canonical model m.

c. R in the Canonical Model Satisfies the Restrictions Specified in Section 5.b of this Chapter. We consider each restriction separately.

(i) For any $X \subseteq W$ and for any $\alpha \in W$, not $R(\alpha,X,\varphi)$.

Assume for reductio that for some $X \subseteq W$ and some $\alpha \in W$, $R(\alpha,X,\varphi)$. By definition of R above, it follows that for some sentences A and B, $|A| = X$, $|B| \subseteq \varphi$, and $O(B/A) \in \alpha$. It follows that $|B| = \varphi$. But $\varphi = |\bot|$, by the definition of $|\bot|$. Hence $|B| = |\bot|$. Therefore $\vdash B \leftrightarrow \bot$.[10] By DR2 we can infer from this last result that $\vdash O(B/A) \leftrightarrow O(\bot/A)$. Since α is maximal and $O(B/A) \in \alpha$, it follows that $O(\bot/A) \in \alpha$. Also by the corollary to Lindenbaum's lemma (hereafter referred to as Cor.) and A2 we know that $\sim O(\bot/A) \in \alpha$. Hence α contains both $O(\bot/A)$ and $\sim O(\bot/A)$. This contradicts the assumption that α is maximal. Hence our initial assumption has led to a contradiction. Therefore, for any $X \subseteq W$, and for any $\alpha \in W$, not $R(\alpha,X,\varphi)$. Q.E.D.

(ii) For any $X, Y \subseteq W$ and for any $\alpha \in W$, if $\alpha \in X$ and $R(\alpha,X,Y)$, then $R(\alpha,W,Y)$.

Let X and Y be any subsets of W and α any member of W such that $\alpha \in X$ and $R(\alpha,X,Y)$. We show that $R(\alpha,W,Y)$.

Since $R(\alpha,X,Y)$, we conclude by the definition of R in the canonical model for some sentences A and B, $|A| = X$, $|B| \subseteq Y$, and $O(B/A) \in \alpha$. By Cor. and A3, we also conclude that $O(B/A) \rightarrow ((A \rightarrow O(B/T)) \in \alpha$. Since α is maximal, it follows from the last two results that $A \rightarrow O(B/T) \in \alpha$. Now we know from above that $\alpha \in |A|$, i.e., that $A \in \alpha$. So $O(B/T) \in \alpha$. We also know that $|T| = W$. Hence there are sentences, namely T and B, such that $|T| = W$, $|B| \subseteq Y$ and $O(B/T) \in \alpha$. Therefore, by the definition of R, $R(\alpha,W,Y)$. Q.E.D.

(iii) For any $X, Y \subseteq W$ and for any $\alpha \in W$, if $R(\alpha,X,Y)$ and $R(\alpha,X',Y')$, then $R(\alpha,X \cup X', Y \cup Y')$.

Let X, X', Y and Y' be any subsets of W and α be any member of W such that $R(\alpha,X,Y)$ and $R(\alpha,X',Y')$. We show that $R(\alpha, X \cup X', Y \cup Y')$.

117

By definition of R there are sentences A and B such that $|A| = X$, $|B| \subseteq Y$ and $O(B/A) \in \alpha$, and there are sentences A' and B' such that $|A'| = X'$, $|B'| \subseteq Y'$ and $O(B'/A') \in \alpha$. By propositional logic,

$\vdash B \to (B \lor B')$ and $\vdash B' \to (B \lor B')$.

By DR1 we infer from $\vdash B \to (B \lor B')$ that $\vdash O(B/A) \to O(B \lor B'/A)$. By Cor., we infer that $O(B/A) \to O(B \lor B'/A) \in \alpha$. Since α is maximal $O(B \lor B'/A) \in \alpha$. From $\vdash B' \to (B \lor B')$ we can derive similarly that $O(B \lor B'/A') \in \alpha$. By A4 and Cor., $O(B \lor B'/A) \land O(B \lor B'/A') \to O(B \lor B'/A \lor A') \in \alpha$. Since $O(B \lor B'/A) \in \alpha$ and $O(B \lor B'/A') \in \alpha$ and since α is maximal $O(B \lor B'/A \lor A') \in \alpha$.

Since $|B| \subseteq Y$ and $|B'| \subseteq Y'$, it follows by set theory that $|B| \cup |B'| = |B \lor B'| \subseteq Y \cup Y'$. Also $X \cup X' = |A| \cup |A'| = |A \lor A'|$. Hence for some sentences, namely $A \lor A'$ and $B \lor B'$, $|A \lor A'| = X \cup X'$, $|B \lor B'| \subseteq Y \cup Y'$ and $O(B \lor B'/A \lor A') \in \alpha$. Hence by the definition of R, $R(\alpha, X \cup X', Y \cup Y')$. Q.E.D.

(iv) For any $X, Y, Y' \subseteq W$ and for any $\alpha \in W$, if $R(\alpha, X, Y)$ and $R(\alpha, X, Y')$, then $R(\alpha, X, Y \cap Y')$.

Let X, Y and Y' be any subsets of W and let α be any member of W such that $R(\alpha, X, Y)$ and $R(\alpha, X, Y')$. We show that $R(\alpha, X, Y \cap Y')$.

By definition of R, there are sentences A, B such that $|A| = X$, $|B| \subseteq Y$ and $O(B/A) \in \alpha$, and there are sentences A', B' such that $|A'| = X$, $|B'| \subseteq Y'$ and $O(B'/A') \in \alpha$. We note that since $|A| = X = |A'|$ by the above, it follows that $|A| = |A'|$, i.e., that $\vdash A \leftrightarrow A'$. By R2, we infer that $\vdash O(B/A) \leftrightarrow O(B/A')$. By Cor. we consequently have $O(B/A) \leftrightarrow O(B/A') \in \alpha$. Since α is maximal, $O(B/A') \in \alpha$.

Furthermore, since $|B| \subseteq Y$ and $|B'| \subseteq Y'$, it follows that $|B| \cap |B'| \subseteq Y \cap Y'$. But $|B| \cap |B'| = |B \land B'|$. Hence $|B \land B'| \subseteq Y \cap Y'$. Since $\vdash (B \land B') \to (B \land B')$ by logic, we let B and B' here be our A and B in R1, and $(B \land B')$ be our D. We infer now that $\vdash [O(B/A') \land O(B'/A')] \to O(B \land B'/A')$. By Cor. it follows that $[O(B/A') \land O(B'/A')] \to O(B \land B'/A') \in \alpha$. But since we have above that $O(B/A') \in \alpha$, and since α is maximal, it follows that $O(B \land B'/A') \in \alpha$.

Therefore, we have now two sentences, namely A' and $(B \land B')$ such that $|A'| = X$, $|B \land B'| \subseteq Y \cap Y'$, and $O(B \land B'/A') \in \alpha$. Hence, by definition of R, we conclude that $R(\alpha, X, Y \cap Y')$. Q.E.D.

By the proof of clauses (i)-(iv) we have established that R as defined in the canonical model m, satisfies all the restrictions mentioned in Section V:5.b and imposed on every model of S. This establishes that our canonical model m is a model for S.

d. A Theorem about m. In Section V:7.a above, a sketch of the completeness proof for S was given. As we stated then, the proof rests on the following theorem which we are now in a position to prove.

Theorem C_0.

Let m be the canonical model for S, then for every sentence A, and every $\alpha \in W$ in m:

$\models^m_\alpha A$ iff $A \in \alpha$.

i.e., $\|A\|^m = |A|$, for every A.

The proof is by induction. We show that the theorem holds of atomic sentences. Then we show that if it holds of sentences B and C it holds of $\bot$, $B \to C$, and $O(C/B)$. This shows that the theorem holds of all sentences of S.

Case (i): Let $A = \mathbb{P}_n$. We need to show that,

$\models^m_\alpha \mathbb{P}_n$ iff $\mathbb{P}_n \in \alpha$.

We know that:

$\models^m_\alpha \mathbb{P}_n$ iff $\alpha \in P_n$

by the definition of truth, clause (i). But by definition of P_n in Section 7.b above $P_n = |\mathbb{P}_n|$. This yields by the definition of $|\mathbb{P}_n|$ that

$$\models_\alpha^m \mathbb{P}_n \text{ iff } \mathbb{P}_n \in \alpha, \text{ for every } \alpha \text{ in m.} \quad \text{Q.E.D.}$$

Case (ii): Let $A = \bot$. We show that for every α

$$\models_\alpha^m \text{ iff } \bot \in \alpha.$$

We know by the definition of truth in Section 5.d above that not $\models_\alpha^m \bot$ for any α in m. Also since each α in m is a maximal set by definition, we conclude by the definition of a maximal set that $\bot \notin \alpha$ for any α in m. Since both $\models_\alpha^m \bot$ and $\bot \in \alpha$ are false for every α in m, the biconditional above follows immediately by elementary logic. Q.E.D.

Case (iii): Let $A = (B \rightarrow C)$. We need to show that for every α in m,

$$\models_\alpha^m B \rightarrow C \text{ iff } B \rightarrow C \in \alpha.$$

Since the proof is by induction, we assume that the theorem holds of B and C and show that it holds of $B \rightarrow C$. By the definition of truth, clause (iii), we have for every α

$$\models_\alpha^m B \rightarrow C \text{ iff if } \models_\alpha^m B, \text{ then } \models_\alpha^m C.$$

But by the inductive hypothesis

$$\models_\alpha^m B \text{ iff } B \in \alpha \text{ and } \models_\alpha^m C \text{ iff } C \in \alpha.$$

Hence, we can conclude by propositional logic that

$$\models_\alpha^m B \rightarrow C \text{ iff if } B \in \alpha, \text{ then } C \in \alpha.\text{[11]}$$

But since α is maximal it follows that

(if B ∈ α, then C ∈ α) iff (B→C) ∈ α.

Hence we have established from the above together with propositional logic that

$\models_\alpha^m$ B→C iff B→C ∈ α.   Q.E.D.

Case (iv): Let A = O(C/B). We need to show that for every α in m

$\models_\alpha^m$ O(C/B) iff O(C/B) ∈ α.

To establish this part we introduce the following lemma.

Lemma.

 Let m be the canonical model for S, and α be any member of W. Then given sentences B and C,

O(C/B) ∈ α iff there are X, Y ⊆ W such that X = |B|, Y ⊆ |C| and R(α,X,Y).

Proof.

(i) From left-to-right.

 We assume O(C/B) ∈ α. By definition of R we need to show that there are sentences B, C such that |B| = X and |C| ⊆ Y and O(C/B) ∈ α. Since we are given above sentences B and C, we let X = |B| and Y = |C|. Together with the original assumption that O(C/B) ∈ α this assignment yields the desired result.

(ii) From right-to-left.

 We assume that there are sets X, Y ⊆ W such that X = |B|, Y ⊆ |C| and R(α,X,Y). We need to show that O(C/B) ∈ α. By definition of R(α,X,Y) we know that there are sentences A' and B' such that |A'| = X, |B'| ⊆ Y and O(B'/A') ∈ α. Also since |A'| = X = |B|, it follows that ⊢A'↔B. Therefore, we can infer by R2 that ⊢O(B'/A')↔O(B'/B). By Cor. 1, it follows that $\vdash O(B'/A') \rightarrow O(B'/B) \in \alpha$. Since α is maximal and since $O(B'/A') \in \alpha$ we know from above, it follows that $O(B'/B) \in \alpha$. Furthermore, since $|B'| \subseteq Y \subseteq |C|$, it follows by set theory that $|B'| \subseteq |C|$. This means that $\vdash B' \rightarrow C$. Hence, by DR1 we can infer that $\vdash O(B'/B) \rightarrow O(C/B) \in \alpha$. Since α is maximal and since $O(B'/B) \in \alpha$ as we know from above, it follows that $O(C/B) \in \alpha$. Q.E.D.

This establishes the lemma.

We now move on to establish case (iv). We assume that the theorem holds of B and C, and show that it holds of $O(C/B)$. By the lemma above,

$O(C/B) \in \alpha$ iff there are sets $X, Y \subseteq W$ such that $X = |B|$, $Y \subseteq |C|$ and $R(\alpha, X, Y)$.

By the inductive hypothesis $|C| = \|C\|^m$ and $|B| = \|B\|^m$. Hence, we can conclude that, $O(C/B) \in \alpha$ iff there are sets $X, Y \subseteq W$ such that $X = \|B\|^m$, $Y \subseteq \|C\|^m$ and $R(\alpha, X, Y)$, which yields directly by clause (iv) of the truth definition that

$O(C/B) \in \alpha$ iff $\models^m_\alpha O(C/B)$. Q.E.D.

The four parts of this inductive proof establish the theorem that $\models^m_\alpha A$ iff $A \in \alpha$ for every sentence A and every $\alpha \in W$ in the canonical model m.

    e. The Completeness Theorem for S.
    If $\models A$, then $\vdash A$.

Proof.

Given Theorem C_0 above, we can now affirm that, and for every sentence A,

$\models^m_\alpha A$ for every α iff $A \in \alpha$, for every α.

But by Cor., we know that

$A \in \alpha$ for every α iff $\vdash A$.

Therefore, we can conclude from the above, that

$\models_\alpha^m$ A for every α iff ⊢A,

i.e.,

$\models^m$ A iff ⊢A.

But now if A is true in every model, then in particular it is true in m, our canonical model. I.e.,

if ⊨A, then $\models^m$ A.

Hence, it follows that

if ⊨ A, then ⊢ A.

I.e., S is complete. Q.E.D.

8. Formulas and Rules not Derivable in S.

In order to give the reader additional insight into S, we list and discuss below some formulas and rules that are not derivable in S. These formulas and rules fall into two categories: (i) those that are independent of S, and (ii) those that are inconsistent with S. The formulas and rules we have chosen in the two categories are ones that we argue against in other parts of this work. Therefore, it is a virtue of S that they are not derivable in it.

a. Formulas and Rules that are Independent of S.

1. O(T/T).

This formula in the logic of conditional obligation corresponds to (A3). (A3) was the one axiom of standard deontic logic which we argued against in Section II:2. In Section V:2 we defined the monadic operator O in terms of the equivalence OA = O(A/T). Consequently, OT = O(T/T). Hence the same reasons for rejecting OT as a theorem prevail for rejecting O(T/T) as a theorem.

To show that $O(T/T)$ is independent of S it is sufficient to show that for some m, α, $\not\vdash_\alpha^m O(T/T)$. By the soundness result for S it follows then that $\not\vdash O(T/T)$. This establishes the desired result.

To show that for some m, α, $\not\vdash_\alpha^m O(T/T)$, let $m_1 = \langle W,R,P \rangle$ where W is any non-empty set, and $R = \varphi$. R^1 satisfies R.1. For suppose it did not, then there would be an $X \subseteq W$ such that $R(\alpha,X,\varphi)$. But $R = \varphi$. Hence R.1 is satisfied. That R.2-R.4 are satisfied is immediately clear since this definition of R makes the antecedent of every restriction R.2-R.4 false. Therefore, it follows by logic that R.2-R.4 are trivially true. Therefore, R satisfies also R.2-R.4.

To show that $\not\vdash_\alpha^{m_1} O(T/T)$, suppose that $\vdash_\alpha^{m_1} O(T/T)$. Then there are sets X, $Y \subseteq W$ such that $R(\alpha, \|T\|, Y)$, $Y \subseteq \|T\|^{m_1}$. But this contradicts our initial assumption that $R = \varphi$. Hence $\not\vdash_\alpha^{m_1} O(T/T)$. Therefore, $\not\vDash O(T/T)$, by definition of $\vDash$. Hence, $\not\vdash O(T/T)$ by the soundness result.

2. $\dfrac{\vdash A}{\vdash O(A/A)}$.

This rule of inference is accepted by van Fraassen in his system of conditional obligation.[12] We reject 2 because it yields $O(T/T)$ as a theorem. That 2 is independent of S follows immediately from the soundness result, logic, and the fact that 2 yields $O(T/T)$.

3. $O(A/C) \to O(A/C \wedge C')$.

This is the principle of augmentation. It is also similar to a theorem in Segerberg's system discussed and rejected in Section III:B:10.d.

To show that 3 is independent of S consider a model $m_2 = \langle W,R,P \rangle$ where $W = \{\alpha\}$, $R = \{\langle \alpha, W, W \rangle\}$ and $P(i) = W$, for $i = 0,1,2,\ldots$. From 3 it follows that

3'. $O(\mathbb{P}_1/\mathbb{P}_1) \to O(\mathbb{P}_1/\mathbb{P}_1 \wedge \sim \mathbb{P}_1)$.

This latter formula is true at α in m_2 exactly when, if $\models_\alpha^{m_2} O(\mathbb{P}_1/\mathbb{P}_1)$, then $\models_\alpha^{m_2} O(\mathbb{P}_1/\mathbb{P}_1 \wedge \sim \mathbb{P}_1)$.

By the definition of truth, the antecedent is true iff there are propositions X, Y $\subseteq$ W such that $R(\alpha,X,Y)$, $Y \subseteq \|\mathbb{P}_1\|^m$ and $X = \|\mathbb{P}_1\|^m$. Clearly such propositions exist; namely, X = Y = W. Hence the antecedent is true. But the consequent is false, since there are no X, Y $\subseteq$ W such that $R(\alpha,X,Y)$ and $X = \|\mathbb{P}_1 \wedge \sim \mathbb{P}_1\| = \varphi$. Therefore, by the definition of truth, `3'` is false. Hence, by the soundness result and logic, 3 is false.

m_2 satisfies restrictions R.1-R.4. That R.1 and R.2 are satisfied is immediately obvious. That R.3 is satisfied follows from the fact that W∪W = W. That R.4 is satisfied follows from the fact that W∩W = W.

b. Formulas that are Inconsistent with S.

1. $O(\perp/\perp)$,

i.e., that under contradictory circumstances, even the impossible is obligatory. We have mentioned earlier that our intuitions are not clear in cases where the circumstances are contradictory. But since A2 was adopted in this system, $O(\perp/\perp)$ becomes inconsistent with S. In Chapter VII we suggest a way for refining A2 with respect to our intuitions, so that the case of contradictory conditions can be treated separately.

2. $O(A/A) \wedge O(A/\sim A) \wedge O(\sim A/A) \wedge O(\sim A/\sim A)$.

It follows at once from this theorem that $O(\perp/\perp)$ which we have shown above to be inconsistent with S. The negation of formula 2 above was introduced by von Wright in his correction of the New System.[13] It is a weakened version of the principle that obligations do not conflict. It was introduced to eliminate the undesirable results deduced by Geach from the New System.[14]

3. $O(A/A)$.

When present as a theorem, this formula rules out immediately statements like "it ought to be the case

that the door is closed, given that the door is open."
Such statements which have the form $O(\sim A/A)$ are often
true though. Statements of the form $O(\sim A/A)$ have
caused a lot of confusion in the literature. We shall
discuss them in detail in Section VI:B:1.

That $O(A/A)$ is inconsistent with S is an immediate
consequence of the fact that it yields $O(\bot/\bot)$ which
is inconsistent with S, as we showed above.

Footnotes

Chapter V

[1] David K. Lewis, <u>Counterfactuals,</u> (Cambridge, Massachusetts: Harvard University Press, 1973), 84.

[2] Ibid., 84-91.

[3] We define:

$\sim A$ as $(A \rightarrow \bot)$
T as $\sim \bot$
$A \wedge B$ as $\sim(A \rightarrow \sim B)$
$A \vee B$ as $(\sim A \rightarrow B)$
$A \leftrightarrow B$ as $[(A \rightarrow B) \wedge (B \rightarrow A)]$.

T represents 'truth'.
$\sim A$ represents 'not A'.
$A \wedge B$ represents 'A and B'.
$A \vee B$ represents 'A or B'.
$A \leftrightarrow B$ represents 'A and B are materially equivalent'.

[4] Georg Henrik von Wright, "A New System of Deontic Logic," <u>Deontic Logic: Introductory and Systematic Readings</u>, ed. Risto Hilpinen (New York: Humanities Press, 1971), 111. Also Bas van Fraassen, "The Logic of Conditional Obligation," <u>Journal of Philosophical Logic</u> 1 (1972), 421.

[5] See for example Hansson's discussion of this point. He opts for a different position. Bengt Hansson, "An Analysis of Some Deontic Logic," Hilpinen, 145.

[6] This becomes immediately obvious when we note that A1 can be replaced by the following three axioms:

a. $A \to (B \to A)$.
b. $[A \to (B \to C)] \to [(A \to B) \to (A \to C)]$.
c. $[(A \to \bot) \to \bot] \to A$.

For this see Krister Segerberg, An Essay in Classical Modal Logic, (Uppsala: Philosophical Studies, 1971), 607.

[7] Ibid.

[8] See G. E. Hughes and M. J. Cresswell, An Introduction to Modal Logic, (London: Methuen and Co., Ltd., 1973), 149-151.

[9] For the proof of this corollary see Appendix 2.

[10] For the proof of this step see Appendix 3.

[11] For the proof of this step see Appendix 2.

[12] van Fraassen, p. 421.

[13] von Wright, 117.

[14] Ibid., 115-116.

CHAPTER VI

SYSTEMS S_1, S_2 AND ALTERNATIVE SEMANTICS FOR S

A. Systems S_1 and S_2

1. Some Additional Axioms.

The system S discussed in Chapter V provides a basis of standard deontic logic which can be enriched by the addition of various intuitive deontic axioms. We now propose some such axioms.

A5. $O(A \wedge B/C) \rightarrow O(A/B \wedge C)$.
A6. $O(A/B \wedge C) \rightarrow [O(A/B) \wedge O(A/C)]$.
A7. $O(A/B \vee C) \rightarrow [\sim B \rightarrow O(A/C)]$.
A8. $[O(A/C) \wedge \sim O(\sim B/C)] \rightarrow O(A/B \wedge C)$.

Note that A5 is derivable from A8 in S by clauses (2) and (5) of the theorem in Section V:4. Several philosophers have found A5 highly intuitive.[1] A5 allows for the possibility that a complex obligation be satisfied in stages, without altering that complex obligation at any stage. Since such an axiom expresses a basic fact about complex obligations, it is the prime candidate for addition to S. The system resulting from the addition of A5-A7 to S will be called here S_1.

A8, though a stronger axiom than A5, is also an intuitive axiom which has already been proposed in the literature.[2] It says that if a state of affairs is permissible, then an obligation remains in force given this state of affairs as a condition. We shall call the system formed by adding A6-A8, S_2. Clearly S_2 is richer than S_1.

Axiom A6 says that if we have an obligation to do A under either conditions B or C, then either we have an obligation to do A under B, or we have an obligation to do A under condition C. This axiom is a weaker version of the converse of A4, the axiom for dilemma. The exact converse of A4 has counter-intuitive consequences. They have been discussed in Section III:10.c.

129

A7 is also a reasonable deontic axiom. It says that if we are obligated to do A in one of two circumstances, one of which does not hold, then it follows that we are obligated to do A given the remaining circumstance.

To validate the axioms of S_1, we must add the restrictions R.5-R.7, listed below, on the relation R in a model for S. To validate the axioms of S_2, we must add restrictions R.6-R.8 instead.

2. Additional Restrictions on R.

R.5 If $R(\alpha, X, Y \cap Y')$, then $R(\alpha, X \cap Y, Y')$.
R.6 If $R(\alpha, X \cup X', Y)$, then $R(\alpha, X, Y)$ or $R(\alpha, X', Y)$.
R.7 If $\alpha \notin X$, then if $R(\alpha, X \cup X', Y)$, then $R(\alpha, X', Y)$.
R.8 If $R(\alpha, X, Y)$ and not $R(\alpha, X, Y')$, then $R(\alpha, X \cap \overline{Y}', Y)$.

In discussing R in Section V:5.b, we explained that we may regard the set Y in $R(\alpha, X, Y)$ as a set of worlds that are deontic alternatives to the world α with respect to condition C defined by the set X. Thus whenever $O(A/B)$ is true at α, then there is a set Y of deontic alternatives to α with respect to condition B, such that A is true at each world in the set Y.

R.5 says that if $Y \cap Y'$ is a set of deontic alternatives to α with respect to X, then Y' is a set of deontic alternatives to α with respect to X and Y. This means that given a condition C and a world α, if we have a complex obligation to fulfill, then fulfilling it in stages, as we almost always do, does not alter the initial set of obligations given α and C. By fulfilling one part of the complex obligation before another, we do not eliminate from consideration ultimately, any component of the original components Y, Y' defining the original set of deontic alternatives. This is as it should be since otherwise the order of fulfilling the obligation becomes deontically significant, which is not the case usually.

Clearly though, in many cases the order in which a complex obligation is fulfilled is indeed important. In such cases we may regard the adherence to such an

order in satisfying the obligation as also obligatory;
or we may regard some specific ways of satisfying the
obligation as impermissible. In either case these
facts are additional premises that restrict further
the sets of deontic alternatives associated with α with
respect to a condition.

R.6 says that if Y is a set of deontic alternatives to a world α with respect to either X or X',
then either Y is a deontic alternative to α with
respect to X or Y is a deontic alternative to α with
respect to X'. This restriction is clear as well as
intuitive.

Restriction R.7 is also obvious. It says that
if the set of deontic alternatives to α with respect
to either condition X or condition X' is Y, and X is
false at α, then one of the set of deontic alternatives
to α with respect to X' alone remains Y.

Finally, R.8 says that if Y is a set of deontic
alternatives to α with respect to the set X, and it is
not the case that Y' is a set of deontic alternatives
to α with respect to X, then Y remains a set of deontic
alternatives to α given X and $\bar{Y}'$. In effect, this
rule asserts that if a state of affairs is permissible
and is brought about, then it should not change our
original obligations; i.e., the original set of
deontic alternatives remains unchanged. This
restriction also is reasonable.

One might object to such a restriction since it
can take us from perfectly acceptable relations
$R(\alpha,X,Y)$ and $R(\alpha,X,Y')$ to $R(\alpha,\varphi,Y)$ wherever $\bar{Y}' \subseteq \bar{X}$.
We have commented in Sections V:3 and V:5.b on
$R(\alpha,\varphi,Y)$, and noted that it can be ruled out in a
richer deontic system.

3. S_1 and S_2 are Sound.

R.5 validates A5, R.6 validates A6, R.7 validates
A7, and R.8 validates A8. To show this we consider
each case separately.

(i) A5 is valid.

To show that $\models O(A \wedge B/C) \rightarrow O(A/B \wedge C)$ it is sufficient to show that for all models m such that R.5 holds, and worlds α in W,

$\models_\alpha^m O(A \wedge B/C) \rightarrow O(A/B \wedge C)$.

Let m be any model, and α any world. Assume that $\models_\alpha^m O(A \wedge B/C)$.

By our assumption and the definition of truth there are sets $X, Y \subseteq W$ such that $R(\alpha, X, Y)$, $Y \subseteq \|A \wedge B\|^m$ and $X = \|C\|^m$. Hence $Y \subseteq \|A\|^m \cap \|B\|^m$. Therefore, there are Y' and Y" such that $Y = Y' \cap Y"$, namely where $Y' = \|B\|^m$ and $Y" = Y$. Since $Y \subseteq \|B\|^m$, it follows that $Y' \cap Y" = Y" = Y$. Also, since $Y \subseteq \|A\|^m$, it follows that $Y' \cap Y" \subseteq \|A\|^m \cap \|B\|^m = \|A \wedge B\|^m$, and that $Y" \subseteq \|A\|^m$. By extensionality of sets, we also infer from the above that $R(\alpha, X, Y' \cap Y")$. Therefore by R.5, $R(\alpha, X \cap Y', Y")$. But $X \cap Y' = \|C\|^m \cap \|B\|^m = \|C \wedge B\|^m$. Hence we have sets, namely $X \cap Y'$ and $Y" \subseteq W$, such that $R(\alpha, X \cap Y', Y")$, $Y" \subseteq \|A\|^m$ and $X \cap Y' = \|C \wedge B\|^m$. Therefore, by the definition of truth, it follows that $\models_\alpha^m O(A/B \wedge C)$. This establishes that

$\models_\alpha^m O(A \wedge B/C) \rightarrow O(A/B \wedge C)$.

Since m and α were arbitrary, the desired result follows. Q.E.D.

(ii) A6 is valid.

Again it is sufficient to show that for all models m and worlds α in W,

$\models_\alpha^m O(A/B \vee C) \rightarrow [O(A/B) \vee O(A/C)]$.

Let m be any model and α any world. It is sufficient by the truth definition to show that if $\models_\alpha^m O(A/B \vee C)$, then $\models_\alpha^m O(A/B) \vee O(A/C)$. We assume that $\models_\alpha^m O(A/B \vee C)$. It follows by the definition of truth that there are $X, Y \subseteq W$ such that $R(\alpha, X, Y)$,

$X = \|B \vee C\|^m$ and $Y \subseteq \|A\|^m$. By R.6 it follows that $R(\alpha, \|B\|^m, Y)$ or $R(\alpha, \|C\|^m, Y)$ since $\|B \vee C\|^m = \|B\|^m \cup \|C\|^m$. It follows from the above that there is a $Y' \subseteq W$ such that either $R(\alpha, \|B\|^m, Y')$ or $R(\alpha, \|C\|^m, Y')$, $Y' \subseteq \|A\|^m$; namely where $Y' = Y$. This means that either there are $X_1, Y_1 \subseteq W$ such that $R(\alpha, X_1, Y_1)$, $Y_1 \subseteq \|A\|^m$ and $X_1 = \|B\|^m$, or that there are $X_2, Y_2 \subseteq W$ such that $R(\alpha, X_2, Y_2)$, $Y_2 \subseteq \|A\|^m$ and $X_2 = \|C\|^m$. Hence by the definition of truth we conclude that $\models_\alpha^m O(A/B) \vee O(A/C)$. Q.E.D.

(iii) A7 is valid.

We show that $\models_\alpha^m O(A/B \vee C) \rightarrow [\sim B \rightarrow O(A/C)]$, for any model m and world α in W. Let m be any model and α any world. It is sufficient by the definition of truth to show that if $\models_\alpha^m O(A/B \vee C)$ and $\models_\alpha^m \sim B$, then $\models_\alpha^m O(A/C)$.

We assume that $\models_\alpha^m O(A/B \vee C)$ and $\models_\alpha^m \sim B$. By the first assumption and the definition of truth, there are sets $X, Y \subseteq W$ such that $R(\alpha, X, Y)$, $X = \|B \vee C\|^m$ and $Y \subseteq \|A\|^m$. By the second assumption $\alpha \not\in \|B\|^m$. Also, $X = \|B \vee C\|^m = \|B\| \cup \|C\|^m$. By R.7 it follows from the above that $R(\alpha, \|C\|^m, Y)$. Hence, there are two sets, namely $\|C\|^m$ and Y such that $R(\alpha, \|C\|^m, Y)$, and $Y \subset \|A\|^m$. Therefore, by the definition of truth $\models_\alpha^m O(A/C)$. Since m and α are arbitrary, this establishes the validity of A7. Q.E.D.

(iv) A8 is valid.

It is sufficient to show that for any model m such that R.8 holds, and world α in W, $\models_\alpha^m [O(A/C) \wedge \sim O(\sim B/C)] \rightarrow O(A/B \wedge C)$. Let m be any model and α any world in m; then it is sufficient to show that if $\models_\alpha^m O(A/C)$ and $\models_\alpha^m \sim O(\sim B/C)$ then $\models_\alpha^m O(A/B \wedge C)$. So we assume that $\models_\alpha^m O(A/C)$ and $\models_\alpha^m \sim O(\sim B/C)$. By the first assumption there are sets $X, Y \subseteq W$ such that $R(\alpha, X, Y)$, $Y \subseteq \|A\|^m$ and $X = \|C\|^m$. By the second assumption it follows that it is false that there is a set $Y' \subseteq W$ such that $R(\alpha, \|C\|^m, Y')$, and $Y' \subseteq \|\bar{B}\|^m$. But clearly $\|\bar{B}\|^m \subseteq \|B\|^m$. Consequently, not $R(\alpha, \|C\|^m, \|\bar{B}\|^m)$. Therefore, by R.8 it follows that $R(\alpha, \|C\|^m \cap \|B\|^m, Y)$, i.e., $R(\alpha, \|B \wedge C\|^m, Y)$. Since $Y \subseteq \|A\|^m$,

we conclude by the definition of truth that
$\models^m_\alpha O(A/B \wedge C)$. Since m and α were chosen arbitrarily, this establishes the validity of A8. Q.E.D.

This concludes the proof of the claim that R.5-R.7 validate axioms A5-A7 in S_1; and that R.6-R.8 validate axioms A6-A8 in S_2.

The systems S_1 and S_2 are richer than S, but could also be enriched in turn in various ways. Further possibilities of enhancing these systems will be suggested in Chapter VII.

B. Alternative Semantics for S.

In Section V:5, we introduced a semantics for S. It is clear from the proofs in the subsequent sections that given such a semantics, the system S is both sound and complete. The axioms and rules of inference of S were motivated and defended in Chapters II and III of this work, as well as in the first part of the present chapter. We would like now to focus discussion on the semantical aspect of S. First, we explore the possibilities of an alternative semantical approach for S. In light of the resulting discussion, we comment in the conclusion of this work on the intuitiveness of the semantics for S, introduced in Section V:5.

In deontic literature, several semantical approaches that are significantly different from ours have been proposed in relation to other deontic logics. We would like to investigate now the possibility that some of these approaches may provide with some modification an acceptable alternative semantics for S.

But before we commence, it is important that we scrutinize a certain formula in deontic logic which we have referred to earlier. This formula has caused confusion in deontic literature, and scrutinizing it will prove to be of great value in our investigation of the various semantical approaches referred to above.

1. $O(\sim A/A)$.

a. Two Different Points of View. In his article "A New System of Deontic Logic," von Wright says:

> Sometimes the world is as it ought to be. It is thoroughly meaningful to make it a duty that O(A/A). The duty to see to it that A when it is the case that A requires us to take heed that the state of affairs in question does not <u>disappear</u>.
> Not always, however, is the world as it ought to be. Then the duty may be that O(A/~A). The duty to see to it that A when this is <u>not</u> the case requires us to take care that the state of affairs in question <u>comes to be</u>.³

On the other hand, Hansson argues in "An Analysis of Some Deontic Logics" that:

> ...I conclude that formulas like O(A/B) shall never be true if A and B are disjoint, if circumstances are taken seriously. And by this I mean, that the circumstances are regarded as something which has actually happened (or will unavoidably happen) and which cannot be changed afterwards.⁴

Van Fraassen follows Hansson. He asserts that ~O(~A/A).⁵ We would like now to examine Hansson's argument for the rejection of O(~A/A), in order to settle this issue. As we shall see later, this issue is very important in our evaluation of the alternative semantics.

b. Hansson's Argument against O(~A/A). Hansson's argument against O(~A/A) consists in offering three unsuccessful readings of O(~A/A), and then concluding on the basis of that failure that no successful reading of O(~A/A) can be given, i.e., a reading which takes conditional obligation seriously and also makes O(~A/A) true.⁶ Of course, it is immediately clear that a successful reading of O(~A/A) can exist even if Hansson did not find it. This renders his argument against O(~A/A) inconclusive, and his statement, which we quoted above, false. But furthermore, we shall show in this section that a successful reading of O(~A/A) can indeed be offered.

(1) The First Reading and Hansson's Notion of "Undoing".

The first reading Hansson offers for O(~A/A) is the following, where A stands for "Smith robs Jones": "Smith ought to refrain from robbing Jones in the circumstance where he actually robs him."[7] Hansson argues against this reading of O(~A/A) on the basis that it is pointless to say any such thing. He argues that Jones cannot "undo" what he already did. Even if Jones restores what he robbed, this is not "undoing" what he did.[8]

The notion of "undoing" used in the argument above involves changing an action which has already been performed into its opposite, not in a subsequent state of affairs but rather at the original state of affairs where that act was performed. It involves a retracing of one's steps in time, back to the moment when the undesirable action was performed and then changing it, and long with it all its consequences. Clearly, such a notion of "undoing" makes it impossible for anyone to "undo" anything which has already been done. As Hansson puts it:

> If Smith has robbed Jones, he cannot 'undo' it. He can restore what he robbed--but this act is not the act of refraining from robbing Jones.[9]

Given this notion of "undoing" and given that "ought" implies "can," the first reading of O(~A/A) which involves this notion of "undoing" does not render O(~A/A) true. Hence, it is not a successful reading.

(2) The Second Reading and the Extra Meaning in O(~A/A).

The second reading of O(~A/A) is given, where A stands for "Smith is smoking in a no-smoking car." It says: If Smith is smoking in a no-smoking car, he ought to stop. Hansson agrees that this reading "sounds good."[10] But nonetheless, he is troubled by it. He explains that,

> ...Dyadic obligations are secondary reparational obligations, telling someone what he should do if he has violated... a primary obligation. Therefore, they should not merely say that the agent should not have done what he did; the primary obligation $O\sim A$ already said that and the situation would be completely described by the mixed formula $A \wedge O\sim A$ if one wants to stress that the agent actually violated the obligation.[11]

In his quest for this extra meaning in $O(\sim A/A)$, Hansson introduces temporal specifications in this third reading. We argue later that temporal specifications are not that extra meaning in $O(\sim A/A)$ which Hansson is looking for. But first, let us comment on the quotation above.

(3) Some Comments on the Second Reading and our Notion of "Undoing".

In Section III:11, as well as in other parts of this work, we provided examples and arguments against the misconception that dyadic obligations are secondary or reparational obligations. We have argued, and in this von Wright concurs,[12] that reparational obligations represent only one part of dydadic obligations. Hence, we disagree with the first part of Hansson's statement. Nevertheless, given our understanding of conditional obligation, we agree with Hansson that $O(\sim A/A)$ must say something more than just $A \wedge O(\sim A)$.

As a matter of fact, our whole discussion of the Conflict-of-Duty Paradox, and then more crucially, the discussion of the paradox of the Contrary-to-Duty Imperative, all go to show that there is an extra meaning in $O(\sim A/A)$ which is not captured by any combination of our usual connectives. This is why a new primitive, $O(/)$, was introduced. In English such a notion of conditionality is differentiated from that of material implication in that while $A \rightarrow O\sim A$ is read as "if A then $O\sim A$," the statement of obligation $O(\sim A/A)$ is read as "given that A, $O\sim A$." The latter reading stresses the fact that $O\sim A$ is conditional upon A, that A is the ground for $O\sim A$. The relation suggested in this second reading cannot be replaced by a conjunction. On the contrary, examples from everyday language rule out such a replacement.

Consider the following statement: Given that the door is closed, it ought to be the case that it is opened. We can easily imagine situations where such a statement which has the form $O(\sim A/A)$ is true, say in a shop where customers sometimes close the door behind them as they leave. Hence, the manager might issue to his salesmen, the instruction above. Consequently, the salesmen are obligated to open the door, whenever it is closed; but the statement itself does not say $(A \wedge O\sim A)$, because in fact, the door is often open. What it does say, though, is that there is a special tie between the circumstance A and the statement of obligation $O\sim A$. This special tie is described by the fact that A is the ground of the obligation expressed by $O\sim A$. Consequently, wherever A is true, the obligation to do $\sim A$ holds.

The example above provides a perfectly legitimate sense of the word "undoing." In this sense a person does not go back in time to reverse an action he has already done. Instead, he reverses this action, if it can be reversed, in the situation in which he finds himself at the time. Hence, an agent who opens a door mistakenly, can perhaps undo his act by closing the door at a later moment. In this sense one can "undo" what he has done; and it is in this perfectly good sense that, say, a seamstress can "undo" her stitches.

(4) The Third Reading and Temporal Specifications.

As we stated earlier, in his quest for the extra meaning of $O(\sim A/A)$, Hansson introduces temporal specifications. He suggests the following reading for (O~A/A), where A stands for "Smith is smoking in a no-smoking car": Now that Smith actually has smoked in a no-smoking car, he ought to refrain from smoking in a no-smoking car. This reading is them amplified into: Now that Smith has smoked in a no-smoking car up to this moment, he ought to refrain from continuing after this moment. Hansson then notes that the last reading fails because it is not of the form O(~A/A).[13]

(5) A Criticism of the Third Reading.

One problem with the last two readings of Hansson is that they say in each case that A is true. As our example in (3) above shows, the notion of conditionality does not require that. It only requires that the dependency of O~A on its ground A, be expressed. Hence, the last two readings say too much.

Secondly, it is worth noting that "now" in each reading is not merely a temporal word; it has two other functions. First, it asserts the fact that Smith has smoked. Such an assertion is, as we argued above, undesirable in the reading of O(~A/A) generally. Second, it ties that fact to the obligation in a tie stronger than that of material implication. Let us show this second point.

Suppose "now" did not express such a strong tie. Then we should be able to replace it by virtue of its first function, with the following reading: Smith has smoked in a no-smoking car up to this moment, and furthermore, if Smith does that, he ought to refrain from continuing after this moment. This reading says merely that A∧OB, according to Hansson. But Hansson argues that O(B/A) says more than just A∧OB. Hence, Hansson, who accepts the third reading, cannot deny this second function of "now" without reducing O(B/A) to saying merely that A∧OB.

As a matter of fact "now" is not unique in being able to fulfill both functions mentioned above. The word "since" does the same. But since we do not want to assert the condition A in the reading of O(~A/A), "since" will not do either. Similarly, the temporal specifications "up to this moment" and "after this moment" are additional information which is unnecessary for explaining the particular meaning of $O(\sim A/A)$, just as it is not necessary for explaining the particular meaning of $A \to OA$.

We conclude that the third reading of $O(\sim A/A)$ given by Hansson, seems acceptable only because "now" in that reading fulfilled among many functions, the function of tying the obligation to its ground. But that function can be fulfilled by the word "given" which has the advantage of not asserting the condition of the obligation. Therefore, we conclude also that our reading of $O(\sim A/A)$ given in (3) above is the correct reading. It says enough, i.e., that A is the condition of $O\sim A$, without saying too much, i.e., that A is true, or that A is true now. It also renders $O(\sim A/A)$ true on certain occasions. This proves false Hansson's conclusion, that $O(\sim A/A)$ can never be true. This result makes us in agreement with von Wright who sees $O(\sim A/A)$ as expressing a duty to bring about $\sim A$, when $\sim A$ is not the case.[14] It also makes it possible to represent obligations like those discussed in Section III:8.

(6) Hansson's Argument has other Consequences.

There is another interesting aspect of Hansson's argument against $O(\sim A/A)$. The same objections to $O(\sim A/A)$ can be redirected against $O(A/A)$ which was proposed by Hansson as an axiom. For example, given Hansson's interpretation of "undoing" presented in Section VI:B:1.b.(1), we can argue not only that an act cannot be "undone", it cannot be "redone" either. This rightly eliminates the first reading. Also, $O(A/A)$ says more than just $A \wedge OA$. This rightly eliminates the second reading. Thirdly, "now that A is actually the case, it ought to be that A" can be stated more carefully according to Hansson as "now that A up to this moment, it ought to be the case that A after this moment." But the latter reading does not have the form $O(A/A)$.

Therefore, Hansson must similarly conclude that far from being an axiom, $O(A/A)$ can never be true.

According to our reading, as well as von Wright's,[15] O(A/A) can be true, namely in cases where A deserved to be preserved.

We are now in a position to consider alternative semantics for S.

2. Lewis' Semantics.

In his book **Counterfactuals**, Lewis introduces a new kind of semantics for the logic of conditional obligation.[16] Using a semantical approach similar to the one he used for the logic of counterfactuals, he introduces the following notions:

A System of Spheres and Spheres.[17]

Let $ be an assignment to each world α of a set $\$_\alpha$ of sets of worlds. Then $ is called a system of spheres, and the members of each $\$_\alpha$ are called spheres around α, if and only if, for each world α, the following conditions hold:

(1) $\$_\alpha$ is nested; that is, whenever S and T belong to $\$_\alpha$, either S is included in T or T included in S.
(2) $\$_\alpha$ is closed under unions.
(3) $\$_\alpha$ is closed under (nonempty) intersections.

In the case of the logic of conditional obligation, this system of spheres is based on comparative goodness of worlds. But as in the case of counterfactuals, the "Limit Assumption" is introduced here too. It basically guarantees that for each A-world α, there exists a smallest A-permitting sphere around α, i.e., a sphere which is morally the best from the point of view of α, given A. An A world is defined as a world in which the fomrula A is true. An A-permitting sphere is defined as a sphere big enought to reach at least one A-world.[18]

The crucial part of this semantics is the definition Lewis offers for O(B/A). He introduces two different versions of O(B/A), namely A□→B and A□⇒B, which differ only in the case where the condition is impossible. The two notions are defined as follows:

> Roughly (under the limit assumption if there are A-worlds evaluable from a world α, then $A\Box\to B$ and $A\Box\Rightarrow B$ are true at α if and only if B holds at all the best A-worlds, according to the ordering [of goodness] from the standpoint of α. More precisely: if there are A-worlds evaluable from α, then they are true at α if and only if some $(A\wedge B)$-world is better, from the standpoint of α, than any $(A\wedge\sim B)$-world.[19]

That this definition is unacceptable should be clear from our lengthy discussion in Section VI:B.1 above. Such a definition rules out cases where the obligation $O(\sim A/A)$ is true. It assumes that the condition of the obligation is preserved after the obligation has been fulfilled. Let us explain in more detail.

Consider the following statement of obligation which is true in the situation described in the previous section: Given that the door is closed, it ought to be the case that the door is open. Let A stand for "the door is closed," and let α be our actual world, i.e., suppose that the situation described above is true in our actual world. It is clear that there are A-worlds evaluable from α. Consequently, the above-mentioned statement of obligation, which has the form $O(\sim A/A)$ is true at α, if and only if some $(A\wedge\sim A)$-world is better, from the standpoint of α, than any $(A\wedge A)$-world, i.e., than any A-world. But an $(A\wedge\sim A)$-world is one in which all moral distinctions collapse. Hence, it cannot be better than any A-world. As a matter of fact, it is not better than α, which is itself an A-world. Hence, by Lewis' definition of $O(B/A)$, $O(\sim A/A)$ can never be true.

But this is not the only problem Lewis' semantics runs into. His definition of comparative permissibility is equally problematics. This notion is directly involved in the definition of $O(B/A)$. It is represented by $A \prec B$, which is read as "it is better that A than that B." In order to determine whether $O(B/A)$ is true at α, we need to determine whether some

(A∧B)-world is better than any (A∧~B)-world. Therefore, if the notion of comparative similarity suffers from some problems, these problems will be ultimately reflected in the definition of O(B/A).

Lewis states that his notion of comparative permissibility is that of comparative goodness at best.[20] He says,

> We may read A◀B as "It is better that A than that B; it is true at α if and only if from the standpoint of α, some evaluable A world is better than any B-world... . Roughly, we are comparing A-at-its-best with B-at-its-best, and ignoring the non-best ways for A and B to hold.[21]

But as we shall show now, this definition leads to counter-intuitive results.

Here is an example which reveals the counter-intuitiveness of this definition. Suppose Andrew is deliberating as to his duties towards his dying mother. Since, there are no extenuating circumstances in this situation, it would seem that his duties consist in spending his time by her side. Let A stand for "Andrew's mother is dying," let B stand for "Andrew stays by his mother's side," and let α be our actual world from which many A-worlds are indeed accessible.

In his deliberation, Andrew concludes that an A-world where he leaves his mother's side to join a team of scientists on a research expedition critical to the survival of all of humanity, etc., has much greater value than any A-world, in which he stays by his mother's side. He concludes that this (A∧~B) world is better than any (A∧B)-world from the point of view of α. Therefore, he asserts on the basis of Lewis' definition, O(~B/A). Andrew then leaves his mother's side with a clear conscience, because he is fulfilling his duty. Only, Andrew does not go on to join the team on its historic expedition because no such team or expedition exist in Andrew's world.

This example illustrates the counter-intuitiveness of Lewis' definition of comparative goodness. That there is a (A∧~B)-world which is better than any (A∧B)-world does not mean that in his world, Andrew's duty is to bring about ~B.

We conclude that if Lewis' semantics is to be acceptable, it has to be modified in two important respects. First, it should allow certain ~A-worlds as well as A-worlds that are evaluable from a certain world α, to participate in determining conditional obligations whose condition is A. Second, it should distinguish between worlds "achievable" from α, and worlds that are not. The latter should play a more limited role, if any, in determining what ought to be the case at α.

3. van Fraassen's Semantics for LC.

In "The Logic of Conditional Obligation," van Fraassen introduces the following semantical approach for his logic of conditional obligation LC.[22] He replaces the notion of accessible worlds with that of attainable states. He also introduces a model structure $\langle K,V,R,f \rangle$ where K and V are non-empty sets, K being the set of attainable states and V being the field of R. R is the relation "greater than" and f is a function that determines the set of values of one world with respect to another. Van Fraassen does not specify what these values are.[23]

The semantics of LC is given by defining its admissible valuations to be exactly the mappings v_α such that α is a member of K and v is a valuation on $\langle K,V,R,f \rangle$. The valuations on $\langle K,V,R,f \rangle$ are defined in the usual way for the propositional connectives. The deontic operator O(A/B), is defined as follows:

$$v_\alpha(O(A/B)) = T \text{ iff } K(A \wedge B) R_\alpha K(\sim A \wedge B)$$

where $K(A) = \{\delta \in K: v\delta(A) = T\}$, and $K(A)R_\alpha K(B)$ exactly if K(A) has a member β such that $\beta R_\alpha \gamma$ for each γ in K(B). $\beta R_\alpha \gamma$, in turn, means that the set of values of β with respect to α, has a member $\underline{u}$ such that u is greater than $\underline{w}$, i.e., $R_\alpha(\underline{u},\underline{w})$, for each $\underline{w}$ in the set of values of γ with respect to α.[24]

Therefore, we can restate the definition of $v_\alpha(O(A/B)) = T$. It is true if and only if there exists an attainable state in which (A∧B) is true and which has, with respect to α, one value in its set of values which is greater than any value in any set of values belonging to any attainable state in which (~A∧B) is true.

The semantics of van Fraassen is open to exactly the same criticisms as those made against Lewis. This semantics does not allow for attainable states where the condition is not preserved. It is incapable of formulating the statement of obligation O(~A/A). As a matter of fact, this semantics as van Fraassen shows, validates ~O(~A/A) as a theorem of the system.[25]

Furthermore, this semantics yields counter-intuitive results as to what ought to be the case in a certain situation. Consider Andrew's situation again in world α. Let A stand for "Andrew's mother is dying," and B for "Andrew stays by his mother's side." $K(A \land \sim B) = \{\delta \in K: v\delta(A) = T\}$. Hence, the ~B-world where Andrew has left his mother to join the team, is a member of K(A∧~B). Since we assumed that this world has the highest moral value with respect to α, i.e., $K(A \land \sim B) R_\alpha K(A \land B)$ it follows again by definition that O(~B/A). This result, as we noted earlier, is counter-intuitive, in cases where no such team exists in α.

Finally, we note that van Fraassen's semantics, as he shows, validates the conditional form of (A3) which we argued against in Chapter II.[26]

RC3 If ⊢ A, then ⊢ O(A/A).

Hence, if van Fraassen's logic is to be acceptable, it has to be modified so that RC3 is no longer valid. Furthermore, it has to allow for the possibility that a ~B-world contributes towards determining conditional obligations whose condition is B. It also needs to distinguish between attainable states simpliciter, and states attainable from α. Consequently, van Fraassen's semantics suffers from basically the same kinds of problems surrounding Lewis' semantics.

4. Other Approaches.

There are two other semantical approaches that are significantly different from ours and which we would like to mention below.

a. The Imperatival Approach. In his article "Values and the Heart's Command," van Fraassen points out several arguments for and against the deontic principle expressed by (A1).[27] We have considered in this work all these arguments in one form or another. Our results were reached, partly, in light of such arguments. Van Fraassen's presentation, which also involves the principle that "ought" implies "can," and the principle expressed by (DR1), i.e., if $\vdash A \rightarrow B$, then $\vdash OA \rightarrow OB$, leads him to different results. He contends that "we already know that no sense can be made of the [three principles] above if we construe what ought to be as what is better or for the best."[28]

In order to make sense of these three principles, van Fraassen appeals to the idea of moral imperatives discussed by Kant, Hegel, Sellars, Castañeda and others.[29] He introduces the notion of an imperative in force, and the notion of an imperative being overridden by another, although he does confess that he does not have an account of how imperatives become in force or how on imperative may override another.[30]

To avoid the problems resulting from the relation of overriding, van Fraassen adopts the thesis that an imperative is not in force if it is overriden. He then limits the scope of his logic of conditional obligation to imperatives in force only. Conditional obligation is defined in terms of conditional imperatives in force only.[31]

We shall not exhibit van Fraassen's semantical approach in greater detail for the following reasons. First, we do not agree that the three principles mentioned previously cannot be made sense of if we construe what ought to be as what is better. Our system S does just that. We emphasize this fact in the conclusion to this work. Secondly, in his effort to avoid paradoxes, van Fraassen is led to distinguish in effect between prima facie and actual imperatives, even though he has no account on which to base such a distinction. If van Fraassen is willing to settle for an unaccounted for distinction, he might have as well introduced one directly with respect to obligations. Nothing is gained by pushing this problem one stage further in his analysis.

Thirdly, the philosophers van Fraassen refers to have proposed the idea of a moral imperative as a basis for the logic of the "ought to do" which is only a part of the logic of the "ought to be."[32] Van Fraassen's attempt at extending this notion to the logic of the "ought to be" is unacceptable in light of statements like "it ought to be the case that everyone is happy." He claims that in such a case the imperative in force is "let everyone be happy." We find such a claim philosophically dubious.

For these reasons, we conclude that van Fraassen's semantical approach does not provide an acceptable alternative to any semantics for S.

b. The Åqvist-type Approach. The only such approach which is capable of handling the paradox of the Contrary-to-Duty Imperative is Åqvist's approach.[33] To resolve this paradox, Åqvist distinguishes between primary and secondary obligations, as we saw earlier in Chapter IV. This distinction succeeds formally in resolving the paradox of the Contrary-to-Duty Imperative. Nevertheless, philosophically, the problem remains with us. It is one and the same moral agent who find himself in a specific moral situation under the two conflicting obligations $O_1 A$ and $O_2 \sim A$. Åqvist does not tell us what course of action the moral agent ought to follow in such cases. Therefore, more information on the relation between primary and secondary obligations must be supplied before this solution becomes acceptable as more than just a formal device for resolving a specific formal problem.

On the other hand, even if we do accept Åqvist's

solution as a successful formal device for resolving the paradox mentioned above, we must note that his system, which is based on this device, leads us into just as serious a paradox. This we discussed in the first part of this chapter. Other formal problems arise from the use of this device in Åqvist's system, as Powers points out.[34] Consequently, the distinction between primary and secondary obligations cannot be justified on formal grounds in Åqvist's system.

Therefore, this approach is in need of major development before it can be considered as a viable candidate for alternative semantics for S.

Footnotes

Chapter VI

[1] For example Bengt Hansson, "An Analysis of Some Deontic Logic," <u>Deontic Logic: Introductory and Systematic Readings,</u> ed. Risto Hilpinen (New York: Humanities Press, 1971), 146.

[2] See for example Hansson, ibid.

[3] Georg Henrik von Wright, "A New System of Deontic Logic," Hilpinen, 110.

[4] Hansson, 142. Emphasis ours.

[5] Bas van Fraassen, "The Logic of Conditional Obligation," <u>Journal of Philosophical Logic</u> 1 (1972), 422.

[6] Hansson, 142.

[7] Ibid.

[8] Ibid.

[9] Ibid.

[10] Ibid.

[11] Ibid.

[12] von Wright, 118-119

[13] Hansson, 142.

[14] von Wright, 110.

[15] Ibid.

[16] David K. Lewis, <u>Counterfactuals,</u> (Cambridge, Massachusetts: Harvard University Press 1973), 97.

[17] Ibid., 96-97.

[18] Ibid., 16.

[19] Ibid., 100.

[20] Ibid., 101.

[21] Ibid.

[22] van Fraassen, 417-438.

[23] Ibid., 425.

[24] Ibid., 426.

[25] Ibid., 422.

[26] Ibid., 421.

[27] van Fraassen, "Values and the Heart's Command," <u>The Journal of Philosophy</u> 70 (1973), 5-19.

[28] Ibid., 15.

[29] Ibid.

[30] Ibid., 15, 17.

[31] Ibid., 17.

[32] See, for example, Hector-Neri Castañeda, "Actions, Imperatives, and Obligations, "<u>Meetings of the Aristotelian Society</u> (October, 1967), 26-47. Also, Sellars, "Reflections on Contrary-to-Duty Imperatives," <u>Nous</u> 1 (1967), 303-344. Note that the statement "John ought to do A" implies the statement "it ought to be the case that John does A."

[33] See our discussion in Section IV:1.b.

[34] Lawrence Powers, "Some Deontic Logicians," <u>Nous</u> 1 (1967), 385-388.

CHAPTER VII

CONCLUSION

The totality of discussions and argumentation in the previous chapters have succeeded in clearing a lot of confusion, and establishing various results in the field of deontic logic. The major accomplishments of this work will be outlined at one point in this chapter.

One result of the discussions and argumentation in this work has been the accumulation of several criteria in accordance with which one can readily evaluate to some extent many deontic logics. To illustrate this fact, we have selected some of the more salient deontic systems for a brief examination below. Our own system S will also be evaluated in light of these criteria.

Once this task is complete, we shall provide a general outline of the contributions of this work, and then close with some suggestions for future deontic research.

1. A Brief Evaluation of the Various Deontic Logics.

   a. von Wright's Systems. As the discussions in this work show, von Wright's Old System is highly intuitive. It captures the basic principles of deontic logic, but it fails to recognize the conditional character of this logic. Consequently, it is incapable of formulating contrary-to-duty imperatives. This fact gives rise to the presence of the paradox of Contrary-to-Duty Imperative. Von Wright's subsequent recognition of this fact and his introduction of the New System to remedy it leads, as showed in Chapter III, to an inconsistency and a false principle. He is thus forced to modify this New System. But, as we showed in Chapter III, while the inconsistency stems from his axiom (B3),

$$\vdash O(A/B \vee C) \leftrightarrow [O(A/B) \wedge O(A/C)],$$

von Wright modifies his New System by rejecting (B1) which expresses in a conditional form the basic deontic principle that obligations do not conflict. The resulting system has two problems: though it is rid of the inconsistency it still has the false principle,

$\vdash O(A/C) \rightarrow O(A/C \wedge {\sim} B).$

It also fails to include the basic deontic principle that obligations do not conflict, and a rule that permits the detachment of an obligation from its conditions.

    b. Hintikka's System. In Chapter IV, we showed that Hintikka's solution to the paradox of the Contrary-to-Duty Imperative does not work. We now show how this paradox can be derived in Hintikka's system. But first we must introduce some notions central to this system. One notion basic to Hintikka's system is that of "satisfiability."[1] Informally, he defines it as the "capability of being true under some state of affairs."[2] Formally, he introduces another notion, namely that of a "model set" in terms of which "satisfiability" is then defined. A "model set" is a formal counterpart of the idea of a partial description of a possible world.[3] The basic idea underlying Hintikka's approach is the following: If we can (partially) construct a possible world in which all the formulae being considered are true, then the set of formulae is satisfiable, i.e., it is mutually consistent.

    A model set μ is formally defined in terms of five basic conditions:[4]

(C.${\sim}$) If $A \in \mu$, then not ${\sim}A \in \mu$.
(C.$\wedge$) If $(A \wedge B) \in \mu$, then $A \in \mu$ and $B \in \mu$.
(C.$\vee$) If $(A \vee B) \in \mu$, then $A \in \mu$ or $B \in \mu$.

and two conditions relating to quantification.

    For sets of formulae involving deontic operators, for example PA, additional conditions are imposed on the model set. These conditions necessitate the consideration of other model sets μ^* (possible worlds) related to μ in a certain way. Hintikka explains that

> This way will be expressed by saying that μ* is a deontic alternative to μ. Intuitively, we may think of μ* as a description of that state of affairs in which A was assumed to be the case for the purpose of showing that it can be the case while all obligations are fulfilled.[5]

Some of these conditions are:[6]

(C.O$^+$) If OA ∈ μ and if μ* is a deontic alternative to μ, then A ∈ μ*.

And:

(C.O*) If OA ∈ μ, then for at least one deontic alternative μ* to μ, A ∈ μ*.

Finally, a set of formulae is satisfiable (consistent, logically possible) if and only if it can be imbedded in a model set μ.[7] We are now ready to derive the Contrary-to-Duty Imperative paradox.

Given the usual premises of this paradox, listed in Chapters II and IV, and assuming as we did before that they are mutually consistent, we can conclude that the set containing exactly this set of premises is satisfiable. But a set of formulae is satisfiable if and only if it can be imbedded in a model set μ. Hence, we can assert on the basis of the above, that the premises of the paradox can all be imbedded in such a set μ. Therefore, where A stands for "Jones robs Smith" and B for "Jones is punished" we have:

(1) A ∈ μ.
(2) O~A ∈ μ.
(3) O(~A→~B) ∈ μ.
(4) (A→OB) ∈ μ.

As we argued earlier, this is the only representation which meets the three adequacy criteria specified in Chapter II. Given this representation, we can conclude that

(5) $OB \in \mu$,

by (1), the definition of $\rightarrow$ and (C.∨). By (C.0*) and (2), we conclude that

(6) $\sim A \in \mu^*$ for some deontic alternative μ^*.

But by (C.0$^+$) and (3), it follows that

(7) $(\sim A \rightarrow \sim B) \in \mu^*$;

and by (C.0$^+$) and (5), it follows that

(8) $B \in \mu^*$.

Hence, by the definition of $\rightarrow$ and (C.∨) we get, together with (6) and (7), that

(9) $\sim B \in \mu^*$.

But this violates condition (C.$\sim$) for the satisfiability of sets. Hence μ^* is not satisfiable. Since deontic alternatives, themselves model sets, must satisfy condition (C.$\sim$), it follows that μ^* is not a deontic alternative to μ. But this result violates condition (C.0*) on the satisfiability of μ. Therefore, μ itself is not satisfiable. This means that the set of premises we imbedded in μ is inconsistent contrary to our original assumption.

This shows that the paradox of the Contrary-to-Duty Imperative has not been resolved in Hintikka's system. Consequently, the system must be modified.

c. Åqvist's System. Unlike Hintikka's system, this one can handle the paradox of the Contrary-to-Duty Imperative. As we said earlier, this is done by introducing a host of deontic operators instead of one. In the last chapter, we mentioned some of the difficulties with this system. Let us summarize them here: First, the system leads to another paradox. Second, the resolution of the original paradox is not satisfactory philosophically. We shall add now that the system contains the rule:[8]

R1. If $\vdash A$, then $\vdash OA$,

which we argued against in Chapter II. Finally, as Powers shows, Åqvist's logic yields the following result:[9] Assuming that a violation has occurred, i.e., $O_1 \sim A$ and A, $A \leftarrow\!\!\rightarrow O_2 A$ for an arbitrary A. These results make Åqvist's system unacceptable.

    d. Hansson's Systems. Hansson introduces three systems in "An Analysis of Some Deontic Logics." As a proponent of the view that $O(\sim A/A)$ can never be true, he includes the following axiom in all of his three systems:[10]

$\vdash O(A/A)$.

He also accepts a conditional version of an axioms we argued against in Chapter II:

$\vdash O(T/A)$.

This axiom is valid in all three systems. Furthermore, Hansson accepts a weaker conditional version of the principle that obligations do not conflict:

$\vdash \sim O(\perp/T)$

which is valid in only two of his systems, DSDL2 and DSDL3. The principle of detaching an obligation from its condition is invalid in all three systems.

    This information about Hansson's systems suffices to make them undesirable for capturing the logic of obligations. Our earlier discussions in Chapter II, III and IV support this conclusion.

    e. Segerberg's System. As we pointed out in Chapter III, this system which validates a theorem to the effect that if one is obliged to do A under condition C, then one is obligated to do A under conditions C and D,[11] can capture at best the logic of absolute or universal obligation. Since absolute obligations are obligations that are actual in every situation, it follows that their logic is a fragment of the logic of actual obligation. Consequently, the logic of absolute obligation is already captured by S. Furthermore, since there are very few, if any, absolute obligations, it follows that the logic of absolute obligation is not very interesting to us, especially in light of more encompassing and useful systems like S. Finally, Segerberg's system includes the objectionable rule:

R2. If ⊢ A, then ⊢ OA.

This makes the system objectionable, even as a logic of absolute obligation.

    f. Lewis' System. In his book <u>Counterfactuals</u>, Lewis does not present an axiom system along with his proposed semantics for a deontic logic. Nevertheless, we have shown in Section VI:B:2 that the formula (O∼A/A) is always false given his semantics. We have argued previously that O(∼A/A) can be true. Consequently, Lewis' semantics provides at least one undesirable result. As we argued in Chapter III, the semantics also provides a counter-intuitive definition of O(A/B).

    g. van Fraassen's Systems. Van Fraassen has proposed two systems of deontic logic. The system introduced in "Values and the Heart's Command," uses the imperatival semantical approach discussed in Chapter VI.[12] In that chapter, we criticized that approach as philosophically dubious since it assumes that every statement of the form O(A/B), including "given C, it ought to be the case that everyone is happy," entails an imperative.

    Furthermore, this system does not permit the detachment of an obligation from its conditions. We have argued in favor of detachment in Chapter IV and showed that van Fraassen's arguments against it were based on a confusion.

    The system also contains as an axiom:

AC2. ⊢ O(A/B) → O(A∧B/B).

In light of our arguments against the claim that $O(\sim A/A)$ is always false, it becomes obvious why we find AC2 objectionable. It says that given an obligation of the form $O(\sim A/A)$, one is under an obligation to do the impossible, given the condition A. Also, the conditional version of the principle that obligations do not conflict is not an axiom of this system. For all these reasons, we find this system unacceptable without major modifications.

Van Fraassen's system introduced in "The Logic of Conditional Obligation" includes the following axioms:[13]

AC2. $\vdash O(A/C) \rightarrow \sim O(\sim A/C)$

and

AC4. $\vdash O(A/B) \rightarrow O(A \wedge B/B)$

and the rule

RC2. If $\vdash A \rightarrow B$, then $\vdash O(A/C) \rightarrow O(B/C)$.

Van Fraassen's system includes also a theorem we find objectionable, namely, $\sim O(\sim A/4)$. The proof for this theorem is given by van Fraassen.[14] It proceeds as follows: Suppose that $O(\sim A/A)$. Then by AC4,

$O(\sim A \wedge A/A)$.

But then by RC2 and logic,

$O(A/A)$.

Hence, by (the second) AC2

$\sim O(\sim A/A)$.

The system also includes

RC3. If $\vdash A$, then $\vdash O(A/A)$

and it does not permit the detachment of an obligation

from its conditions. In Chapter VI, we already provided a criticism of the semantics of this system. Consequently, for all these reasons, we find van Fraassen's second system unacceptable.

h. Mott's System. Mott's system suffers from problems similar to those of systems that we have already discussed. It contains the rule[15]

(RD) from ⊢ A infer ⊢ OA

which yields immediately the objectionable theorem OT.

Mott's system unlike those of von Wright, Hansson and others, does not treat conditional obligation as a primitive notion. Hence, his system includes for example:[16]

(A8) ⊢ (~A⊐→A)→OA,

which we find highly counter-intuitive in light of a modified version of the example presented in Section VI:B:1.b.(3). We modify the example so that the door opens whenever it is closed because it has a spring attached to it. In such a case, no obligation to open the door can be inferred from the facts of this situation.

On the other hand, Mott's system does include an axiom expressing the principle that obligations do not conflict, and another permitting the detachment of an obligation from its conditions. Yet, in light of the criticisms above, Mott's system is unacceptable.

Other systems of deontic logic which have not been considered above, can be evaluated similarly in light of the criteria proposed at various points in this work.

2. A Brief Evaluation of S.

In Section 1, we presented a very condensed criticism of various deontic systems. The criticisms were based on criteria that were developed in the body of this text. We now evaluate the system S in light of the same criteria.

It is clear that in S the following is not a rule. If ⊢ A, then ⊢ OA. As a matter of fact, our semantics was chosen carefully so as not to validate this principle. Furthermore, the basic concepts of deontic logic are all present including the principle that obligations do not conflict. Also, the system permits via axiom A3 the detachment of an obligation from its conditions.

The formula O(~A/A) holds its proper position in S as a contingent statement, and the dyadic deontic operator is regarded as a primitive and not as a complex entity. As such S is not open to the criticism directed at the end of the previous section against other systems of conditional obligation.

Furthermore, the semantics developed for S is intuitive. In the case of O(B/A), the relation R used in the definition of truth for O(B/A) at α can be regarded as a relation which picks out a collection of sets of worlds that are the "best achievable worlds from α with respect to condition A." Where such worlds exist and B is true in each of them, O(B/A) is regarded as true.

We use the expression "achievable from α" in the same sense we used this expression in Chapter VI. It refers to a set of worlds that not only are possible, but also possible to attain from α. For example, a world in which a person called Joe is happy and well, though possible is not achievable from α where α is a world in which Joe has already died. That R picks out, whenever it is not empty, a collection of sets of worlds with respect to condition A from the set of worlds achievable from α removes the possibility of counter-intuitive results of the sort present in Lewis' and van Fraassen's system.

Also, our treatment of the major principles of deontic logic and the related paradoxes has resulted in a paradox-free system S. This system falsifies van Fraassen's claim that no sense can be made of the above-mentioned principles while construing what ought

to be as what is for the best.17 Clearly, since R
picks out a collection of the best worlds of a certain
set, the semantics of S construes what ought to be as
what is for the best. This is in accordance with
most intuitions as to what "ought" means.

We conclude that S meets all the criteria of
evaluating a deontic system that were presented in the
previous section.

3. A Summary Statement on the Value of this Work.

This work is mainly concerned with the defense
of the most basic deontic principles that have become
suspect as a result of the paradoxes of deontic logic.
In this work, we have succeeded in resolving the
paradoxes while retaining those basic deontic principles in a conditional form in the system S.

The systematic study of the problems arising from
the paradoxes revealed and cleared a lot of confusion
in the field, for example, with respect to the
principle of detaching the obligation from its
conditions. But to achieve these results a thorough
investigation of the philosophical foundations of
deontic logic became necessary. The notions of prima
facie and actual obligation were presented and
developed. Traditional counter-examples against the
standard deontic principles were consequently
examined and dismissed with the help of these developed
notions.

As a result, many deontic systems were found
unacceptable. These systems in their attempts to cope
with the problems of deontic logic reached unacceptable conclusions that were reflected in their systems.
Wherever arguments were supplied for such conclusions,
the conclusions were evaluated.

The paradox which was most enlightening as to the
philosophical foundations of deontic logic turned out
to be the Conflict-of-Duty paradox. It revealed that
the proper scope of deontic logic is that of actual
obligations. On the other hand, it was the paradox
of the Contrary-to-Duty imperative that finally made

it necessary to introduce a major formal modification of von Wright's Old System of deontic logic which contains all the basic principles.

As the investigation proceeded, another logic, the logic of prima facie obligation or presumptions took shape in front of us. Although we found out a lot about this logic which is closely related to deontic logic, the results were not formalized because they fall outside the scope of this work.

The result of this inquiry is finally a paradox-free intuitive logic which preserved all the basic deontic principles. This logic is being proposed as the correct standard deontic logic to replace von Wright's Old System. Now that this standard logic has been established, it presents many possibilities for further developments. We discuss those now.

4. Suggestions for Further Research.

One important way to develop S is by adding to it an appropriate alethic modal system. This step is not superfluous. On the contrary, it resolves an important problem with respect to S and other deontic systems, namely, the problem of the case where $A = \bot$ in the axiom:

$\vdash \sim O(\bot/A)$.

This problem is averted altogether when an appropriate alethic modal system is introduced. The above axiom can then be expressed as

$\vdash \Diamond A \rightarrow \sim O(\bot/A)$.

This accords perfectly with our intuitions.

Another problem is that of iterated modalities. The semantics proposed for S can handle iterated modalities. But the philosophical aspects of such a problem are quite interesting. Also, there is the question related to these philosophical aspects, as to whether we need a reiterated dyadic deontic operator, or a monadic one in whose scope the dyadic operator falls. Both possibilities are logically, as well as philosophically, interesting.

The question of whether the dyadic operator $O(/)$ is complex or not must be investigated further. More arguments must be developed in this area. The similarities between the problems of deontic logic and other fields, for example, that of scientific explanation, might shed some interesting light on this question.

Finally, additional formulae expressing the interaction between the circumstance and the obligation may be explored and added to our standard deontic logic. Hansson lists several such formulae in his article "An Analysis of Some Deontic Logics," for example:[18]

$$\vdash O(A/B \wedge C) \rightarrow O(A \vee \sim B/C)$$

and

$$\vdash O(A \vee B/C) \leftrightarrow [O(A/C) \vee O(B/C \wedge \sim A)].$$

He also lists

$$\vdash [O(A \vee B/C) \wedge \sim O(A/C)] \rightarrow O(B/C \wedge \sim A).$$

These are some suggestions for future research in this area.

Footnotes

Chapter VII

[1] Jaakko Hintikka, "Some Main Problems of Deontic Logic," <u>Deontic Logic: Introductory and Systematic Readings</u>. ed. Risto Hilpinen (New York: Humanities Press, 1971), 68.

[2] Ibid., 63.

[3] Ibid.

[4] Ibid., 68.

[5] Ibid., 70.

[6] Ibid., 72, 70.

[7] Ibid., 68.

[8] Lennart Åqvist, "Good Samaritans, Contrary-to-Duty Imperatives, and Epistemic Obligations," <u>Nous</u> 1 (1967), 362.

[9] Lawrence Powers, "Some Deontic Logicians," <u>Nous</u> 1 (1967), 362.

[10] Bengt Hansson, "An Analysis of Some Deontic Logics," <u>Deontic Logic: Introductory and Systematic Readings</u>, ed. Risto Hilpinen (New York: Humanities Press, 1971), 144.

[11] Krister Segerberg, "Some Logics of Commitment and Obligation," Hilpinen, 148-156. Note that the "if...then--" in this statement is not that of material implication.

[12] Bas van Fraassen, "Values and the Heart's Command," <u>Journal of Philosophy</u> 1 (1973), 5-19.

[13] Bas van Fraassen, "The Logic of Conditional Obligation," <u>Journal of Philosophical Logic</u> 1 (1972), 421-422.

[14] Ibid., 422.

[15] P. Mott, "On Chisholm's Paradox," <u>Journal of Philosophical Logic</u> 2 (1973), 198.

[16] Ibid., 208.

[17] van Fraassen, "Values", 15.

[18] Hansson, 145-146.

APPENDIX 1

The Axiom Schemas and Rules of Inference for S.

A1. $\vdash$ A, if A is a tautology.

A2. $\vdash \sim O(\bot/C)$.

A3. $\vdash O(B/A) \to (A \to O(B/T))$.

A4. $\vdash [O(B/A) \land O(B/A')] \to O(B/A \lor A')$.

R1. $\dfrac{\vdash (A \land B) \to D}{\vdash [O(A/C) \land O(B/C)] \to O(D/C)}$.

R2. $\dfrac{\vdash A \leftrightarrow A'}{\vdash O(B/A) \leftrightarrow O(B/A')}$.

Derived Rules of S.

DR1 $\dfrac{\vdash A \to B}{\vdash O(A/C) \to O(B/C)}$.

DR2 $\dfrac{\vdash A \leftrightarrow B}{\vdash O(A/C) \leftrightarrow O(B/C)}$.

Restrictions on R in a model for S.

R1. Not $R(\alpha, X, \varphi)$.
R2. If $\alpha \in X$ and $R(\alpha, X, Y)$, then $R(\alpha, W, Y)$.
R3. If $R(\alpha, X, Y)$ and $R(\alpha, X', Y')$, then $R(\alpha, X \cup X', Y \cup Y')$.
R4. If $R(\alpha, X, Y)$ and $R(\alpha, X, Y')$, then $R(\alpha, X, Y \cap Y')$.

The Notion of Truth at α in m is Defined as Follows.

(i) $\models^m_\alpha \mathbb{P}_n$ iff $\alpha \in P_n$, for any n;

(ii) not $\models^m_\alpha$;

(iii) $\models^m_\alpha A \to B$ iff if $\models^m_\alpha A$, then $\models^m_\alpha B$;

(iv) $\models^m_\alpha O(B/A)$ iff there are X, Y $\subseteq$ W such that

165

$R(\alpha,X,Y)$, $Y \subseteq \|B\|^m$ and $X = \|A\|^m$.

In a Canonical Model m.

$R(\alpha,X,Y)$ iff for some sentences A, B, $|A| = X$, $|B| \subseteq Y$ and $O(B/A) \in \alpha$

and

$P_n = |\mathbf{P}_n|$

where $|A|$ = the class of all maximally consistent set of sentences in S containing the sentence A.

APPENDIX 2

Some Properties of Maximal Sets.

If α is a maximal set, then

(1) $\alpha \vdash A$ iff $A \in \alpha$.
(2) $\sim A \in \alpha$ iff $A \notin \alpha$.
(3) $A \rightarrow B \in \alpha$ iff if $A \in \alpha$, then $B \in \alpha$.

We shall show (1) only. The proofs for (2) and (3) can be easily constructed from the proofs given in G. E. Hughes and M. J. Cresswell, <u>An Introduction to Modal Logic</u>, (London: Methuen & Co., 1973), 151-154.

Proof of (1).

(i) Left-to-right.

Assume that $\alpha \vdash A$ and show that $A \in \alpha$. To show $A \in \alpha$ we assume for reductio that $A \notin \alpha$. Therefore by (2), $\sim A \in \alpha$. Hence $\alpha \vdash \sim A$ by definition of $\vdash$. Hence $\alpha \vdash A \wedge \sim A$ by definition of $\vdash$ and the above, i.e., α is not consistent, which contradicts the assumption that α is maximal. Hence, $A \in \alpha$.

(ii) Right-to-left.

Trivial.

Corollary to Lindenbaum's Lemma.

$\vdash A$ iff for all maximal sets α, $A \in \alpha$.

Proof.

(i) Left-to-right.

Suppose $\vdash A$, then by definition of $\vdash$, it follows that $\alpha \vdash A$ for all maximal sets α. Therefore, by (1) above $A \in \alpha$ for all maximal sets α.

(ii) Right-to-left.

Suppose $\not\vdash$ A. Then $\{\sim A\} \not\vdash \bot$. Hence by Lindenbaum's lemma there is a maximal extension α of $\{\sim A\}$. Hence A ∉ α, by the maximality of α. Therefore there is a maximal set α such that A ∉ α. Therefore, it is not the case that for all α, A ∈ α. Q.E.D.

APPENDIX 3

Lemma.

If $|A| = |A'|$, then $\vdash A \leftrightarrow A'$.

Proof.

By definition of $|A|$ and $|A'|$, we have that $\{\alpha: A \in \alpha\} = \{\alpha: A' \in \alpha\}$; i.e., for all maximal sets α, $A \in \alpha$ iff $A' \in \alpha$. Therefore, by familiar properties of maximal sets $A \leftrightarrow A' \in \alpha$, for every maximal set α. This means by (1) in Appendix 2 that $\vdash A \leftrightarrow A'$.

BIBLIOGRAPHY

Anderson, Alan Ross. "A Reduction of Deontic Logic to Alethic Modal Logic." Mind 67 (1958), 100-103.

_____. "Some Nasty Problems in the Formal Logic of Ethics." Nous 1 (1967), 345-360.

Åqvist, Lennart, "Good Samaritans, Contrary-to-Duty Imperatives, and Epistemic Obligations." Nous 1 (1967), 361-379.

Baier, Kurt. The Moral Point of View. New York: Random House, 1966.

Beatty, Harry. "On Evaluating Deontic Logic." Journal of Philosophical Logic 1 (1972), 439-444.

Becker, Lawrence C. On Justifying Moral Judgments. New York: Humanities Press, 1973.

Castañeda, Hector-Neri. "Actions, Imperatives and Obligations." Meeting of the Aristotelian Society, London, October 1967, 25-48.

_____. "Acts, the Logic of Obligation, and Deontic Calculi." Critica 1 (1967), 77-95.

_____. "The Logic of Change, Action, and Norms." Journal of Philosophy 62 (1965), 333-344.

_____. "The Logic of Obligation." Philosophical Studies 10 (1950), 62-75.

_____. "A Theory of Morality." Philosophy and Phenomenological Research 17 (1957), 339-352.

Chellas, Brian F. "Basic Conditional Logic." Forthcoming in the Journal of Philosophical Logic.

_____. "Conditional Obligation." Logical Theory and Semantic Analysis: Essays Dedicated to Stig Kanger on His Fiftieth Birthday. Ed.

Sören Stenlund. Dordrecht: D. Reidel Publishing Co., 1974, 23-33.

_____. *The Logical Form of Imperatives*. Stanford: Perry Lane Press, 1969.

_____. "The Story of O." Paper read at the Meetings of the American Philosophical Association, Chicago, 1974.

Chisholm, Roderick M. "Contrary-to-Duty Imperatives and Deontic Logic." *Analysis* 24 (1963), 33-36.

Cox, Azizah al-Hibri, "A Critical Survey in Deontic Logic." Unpublished Master's thesis, Detroit: Wayne State University, 1968.

Danielson, Sven. "On Strength of Commitments." *Modality, Morality and Other Problems of Sense and Nonsense Essays Dedicated to Sören Halldén*. Lund, Sweden: C. W. K. Gleerup Bokforlag, 1973.

Feinberg, Joel. *Moral Concepts*. Oxford: Oxford University Press, 1970.

Føllesdal, Dagfinn and Risto Hilpinen. "Deontic Logic: An Introduction." *Deontic Logic: Introductory and Systematic Readings*. Ed. Risto Hilpinen. New York: Humanities Press, 1971, 1-35.

Hansson, Bengt. "An Analysis of Some Deontic Logics." *Deontic Logic: Introductory and Systematic Readings*. Ed. Risto Hilpinen. New York: Humanities Press, 1971, 121-147.

Hare, R. M. *Freedom and Reason*. Oxford: The Clarendon Press, 1963.

_____. *The Language of Morals*. Oxford: The Clarendon Press, 1952.

Hilpinen, Risto, ed. *Deontic Logic: Introductory and Systematic Readings*. New York: Humanities Press, 1971.

Hintikka, Jaakko. "Some Main Problems of Deontic Logic." *Deontic Logic: Introductory and Systematic Readings*. Ed. Risto Hilpinen. New York: Humanities Press, 1971, 59-104.

Hughes, G. E. and M. J. Cresswell. *An Introduction to Modal Logic*. London: Methuen and Co., Ltd., 1973.

Kripke, Saul A. "A Completeness Theorem in Modal Logic." *The Journal of Symbolic Logic* 24 (1959), 1-14.

Lemmon, E. J. "Deontic Logic and the Logic of Imperatives." *Logique et Analyse*, n.s., 29 (1965), 39-71.

——————. "Moral Dilemmas." *Philosophical Review* 71 (1962), 139-158.

Lewis, David K. *Counterfactuals*. Cambridge: Harvard University Press, 1973.

Mally, Ernst. *Grundgesetze des Sollens: Elemente de Logik der Willens*. Graz: Leuschner and Lubensky, 1926.

Melden, A. I., ed. *Essays in Moral Philosophy*. Seattle: University of Washington Press, 1958.

Mill, John Stuart. *Utilitarianism*. New York: E. Dutton & Co., 1910.

Mott, Peter L. "On Chisholm's Paradox." *Journal of Philosophical Logic* 2 (1973), 197-211.

Nowell-Smith, P. H. and E. J. Lemmon. "Escapism: The Logical Basis of Ethics." *Mind* 69 (1960), 289-300.

O'Connor, D. J. *Free Will*. New York: Anchor, 1971.

Paton, H. J. *The Moral Law*. New York: Barnes and Noble, 1950.

Powers, Lawrence. "Some Deontic Logicians." *Nous* 1

(1967), 381-400.

Prior, A. N. "Escapism: The Logical Basis of Ethics." *Essays in Moral Philosophy*. Ed. A. I. Melden. Seattle: University of Washington Press, 1958, 135-146.

_____. "The Paradoxes of Derived Obligation." *Mind* 63 (1954), 64-65.

Quine, W. V. "The Ways of Paradox." *The Ways of Paradox and Other Essays*. New York: Random House, 1966.

Rees, W. J. "Moral Rules and the Analysis of 'Ought'." *Philosophical Review* 62 (1953), 23-40.

Rickman, H. P. "Escapism: The Logical Basis of Ethics." *Mind* 72 (1963), 273-274.

Robison, John. "Who, What, Where and When: A Note on Deontic Logic." *Philosophical Studies* 15 (1964), 89-92.

Ross, Alf. "Imperatives and Logic," *Theoria* 7 (1941), 53-71.

Ross, W. David. *The Foundations of Ethics*. Oxford: Oxford Press, 1939.

_____. *The Right and the Good*. Oxford: The Clarendon Press, 1930.

Sartre Jean-Paul. *Existentialism is a Humanism*. Translated by Philip Mairet. London: Methuen & Co., 1948.

Segerberg, Krister. *An Essay in Classical Modal Logic*. Uppsala: Philosophical Studies, 1971.

_____. "Some Logics of Commitment and Obligation." *Deontic Logic: Introductory and Systematic Readings*. Ed. Risto Hilpinen. New York: Humanities Press, 1971, 148-158.

Sellars, Wilfrid. "Reflections on Contrary-to-Duty Imperatives." Nous 1 (1967), 303-344.

Stalnaker, Robert C. and Richmond H. Thomason. "A Semantic Analysis of Conditional Logic." Theoria 36 (1970), 23-42.

Thomason, Richmond H. "Deontic Logic as Founded on Tense Logic." Draft of a talk presented at the Temple University Conference on Deviant Semantics, December, 1970.

van Fraassen, Bas. "The Logic of Conditional Obligation." Journal of Philosophical Logic 1 (1972), 417-438.

_____. "Values and the Heart's Command." Journal of Philosophy 70 (1973), 5-19.

von Wright, Georg Henrik. "A Correction to a New System of Deontic Logic." Danish Yearbook of Philosophy 2 (1965), 103-107.

_____. "Deontic Logic." Mind 60 (1951), 1-15.

_____. "A New System of Deontic Logic." Danish Yearbook of Philosophy 1 (1964), 173-182. Also reprinted in Deontic Logic: Introductory and Systematic Readings. Ed. by Risto Hilpinen. New York: Humanities Press, 1971, 105-120.

_____. Norm and Action. London: Routledge and Kegan Paul, 1963.

_____. "A Note on Deontic Logic and Derived Obligation." Mind 65 (1951), 507-509.

Wolff, Robert Paul. The Autonomy of Reason. New York: Harper and Row, 1973.

INDEX

Affairs, generic state of 9
Anderson, Allan Ross 17
Anderson simplification, the 17, 41, 42
Åqvist, Lennart 23, 29, 42, 81, 82, 84, 91-94, 147
    148, 154, 155

Baier, Kurt 45
Beatty, Harry 38-40

Castañeda, Hector-Neri 45, 54-59, 82, 146
Chellas, Brian F. 20
Chisholm, Roderick 1, 27, 78, 95, 96, 97, 101
Cox, Azizah al-Hibri 17, 41

Equivalents
  provable 10, 11
  tautological 10, 11

Føllesdal, Dagfinn 15

Geach, P T. 79, 125
Goodness, comparative 141, 143, 144

Hansson, Bengt 13, 14, 15, 21, 31, 41, 80, 84, 90,
    94, 96, 97, 135, 136-138, 139-141, 155, 158, 162
Hare, R. M. 52, 53, 54, 59, 60
Hegel, Georg Wilhelm Friedrich 146
Hilpinen, Risto 15
Hintikka, Jaakko 29, 32-35, 76-78, 82, 84, 90-91,
    96, 152, 153, 154

Imperatives
  actual 147
  prima facie 147

Kant, Immanuel 146

Laws
  of commitment 13
  for the dissolution of deontic operators 13

Lemmon, E. J. 17, 21, 25, 42, 45, 49, 52, 53
Lewis, David 5, 102, 141, 141, 144, 156, 159
Limit assumption, the 141
Lindenbaum's lemma 115

Mally, Ernst 1
Mill, John Stuart 59
Mott, Peter L. 26, 95-97, 158

New System 1, 14, 78, 80, 94, 106, 125, 151
  definition of 78
Nowell-Smith, P. H. 17, 21, 42

Obligations
  absolute 64, 155
  actual (see ought-statements, actual)
  conditional 2, 63, 72, 94, 97, 141
  prima facie (see ought-statements, prima facie)
  primary 42
  reparational 91
  secondary 42, 91
  universal 82, 155
Old system 9, 10, 11, 14, 94, 105, 106, 151, 161
  definition of 14
Ought statements
  actual 4, 46-60, 51-52, 53, 61, 62, 64, 66, 67,
      70, 72, 74, 75, 76, 78, 82, 84, 92, 93, 104,
      155, 160
  prima facie 4, 46, 50, 51-53, 55, 61, 62-67, 69-70,
      72-74, 75-78, 81-84, 92, 93, 104, 160, 161

Paradox 1, 2, 3, 20, 21, 22, 31
  Åqvist 23, 29,
  Conflict-of-Duty, the 2, 4, 6, 29, 30, 32, 76, 78
  Contrary-to-Duty Imperative 1, 2, 4, 26, 30, 32, 78,
    89, 91, 92, 94, 137, 141, 151, 153, 154, 160
  Epistemic obligation, the 28, 30
  Good Samaritan, the 2, 3, 23, 29, 30, 32, 41-43
  Plato's 24, 25, 29, 30, 45, 48, 49, 50, 51, 53,
    56, 61
  Robber's, the 24, 29, 42
  Ross' 2, 3, 22, 30, 32, 37-38, 40, 41
  Russell's 21
  Sartre's 25, 29, 30, 59, 61, 64, 68, 70, 71-73, 75,
    76

Victim's, the 24, 29, 42

The author was born in Beirut Lebanon, 1943. She received her undergraduate education at the American University of Beirut. In 1966 she came to the U.S. where she pursued her education at Wayne State University in Detroit. She was awarded a masters degree in 1968. The author then attended Indiana University and later the University of Pennsylvania. She was awarded a doctorate degree in Philosophy from the University of Pennsylvania in 1975. Since the beginning of her graduate work the author was particularly interested in deontic logic. Most of her research now is in that field. Other areas that are also of interest to her are political theory, Philosophy of Technology in which she is co-editing an anthology, and the philosophy of feminism. At the present, she is an assistant professor of philosophy at Texas A&M University.